Easy
Baking

THE AUSTRALIAN
Women's Weekly

contents

Baking is back, and we're happy about that, but there's been a quiet revolution in the area of cake pans – the material they're made from, the widths, depths, and even the shapes, have changed. If you're a new baker you need to read the information in this book on cake pans. If you are an experienced baker, you'll cope with the new or the old cake pans, but you should still read the information.

Pamela Clark

Food director

Baking for the cake stall

Small cakes, big cakes, biscuits, slices, brownies, cupcakes

orange blossom cakes

100g butter, softened

1 teaspoon orange blossom water

½ cup (110g) caster sugar

2 eggs

1 cup (150g) self-raising flour

¼ cup (30g) almond meal

½ cup (125ml) milk

ORANGE BLOSSOM GLACÉ ICING

1 cup (160g) icing sugar

10g softened butter

1 teaspoon orange blossom water

1 tablespoon water, approximately

1 Preheat oven to 180°C/160°C fan-forced. Grease six-hole (¾-cup/180ml) mini fluted tube pan or texas muffin pan.

2 Beat butter, blossom water and sugar in small bowl with electric mixer until light and fluffy. Beat in eggs, one at a time (mixture will curdle). Stir in sifted flour, meal and milk, in two batches.

3 Divide mixture into pan holes; bake about 25 minutes. Stand cakes in pan 5 minutes before turning, top-side up, onto wire rack to cool.

4 Meanwhile, make orange blossom glacé icing. Drizzle icing over cakes.

orange blossom glacé icing Sift icing sugar into small heatproof bowl; stir in butter, blossom water and enough of the boiling water to make a firm paste. Stir over small saucepan of simmering water until icing is pourable.

prep + cook time 45 minutes **makes 6**

note Orange blossom water is a concentrated flavouring made from orange blossoms; it is available from Middle-Eastern food stores, some supermarkets and delicatessens. Citrus flavourings are very different.

mini sultana loaves

125g butter, melted

2⅓ cups (375g) sultanas

⅔ cup (150g) caster sugar

2 eggs

⅓ cup (80ml) buttermilk

½ cup (75g) plain flour

¾ cup (110g) self-raising flour

LEMON GLACÉ ICING

1½ cups (240g) icing sugar

20g softened butter

2 tablespoons lemon juice, approximately

1 Preheat oven to 160°C/140°C fan-forced. Grease 8-hole (¾-cup/180ml) petite loaf pan.

2 Stir ingredients in large bowl with wooden spoon until combined.

3 Divide mixture into pan holes, smooth tops; bake about 30 minutes. Stand cakes 5 minutes before turning, top-side up, onto wire rack to cool.

4 Meanwhile, make lemon glacé icing. Drizzle icing over cakes.

lemon glacé icing Sift icing sugar into small heatproof bowl; stir in butter and enough juice to make a firm paste. Stir over small saucepan of simmering water until icing is pourable.

prep + cook time 55 minutes **makes** 8

fig baklava

1 cup (160g) roasted blanched almonds
1 cup (140g) roasted unsalted pistachios
1 cup (170g) coarsely chopped dried figs
2 teaspoons ground cinnamon
1 teaspoon ground clove
1 teaspoon ground nutmeg
9 sheets fillo pastry
80g butter, melted
HONEY SYRUP
1 cup (250ml) water
¾ cup (165g) caster sugar
⅓ cup (115g) honey
1 teaspoon finely grated lemon rind

1 Preheat oven to 200°C/180°C fan-forced. Grease deep 22cm-square cake pan.

2 Blend or process nuts, figs and spices until chopped finely.

3 Cut pastry sheets in half crossways. Layer three pastry squares, brushing each sheet with butter; place in pan, sprinkle with ½ cup of the nut mixture. Repeat layering with remaining pastry, butter and nut mixture, ending with pastry.

4 Cut baklava into quarters; cut each quarter into four triangles. Bake 25 minutes.

5 Reduce oven temperature to 150°C/130°C fan-forced; bake baklava a further 10 minutes.

6 Meanwhile, combine ingredients for honey syrup in small saucepan. Stir over heat until sugar dissolves; bring to the boil. Reduce heat; simmer, uncovered, without stirring, for 10 minutes.

7 Pour hot syrup over hot baklava; cool in pan.

prep + cook time 55 minutes **makes** 16

chocolate raspberry brownies

150g butter, chopped coarsely

350g dark eating chocolate, chopped coarsely

1 cup (220g) caster sugar

2 eggs

1¼ cups (185g) plain flour

½ cup (75g) self-raising flour

200g fresh or frozen raspberries

2 teaspoons cocoa powder

1 Preheat oven to 180°C/160°C fan-forced. Grease deep 20cm-square cake pan; line base and sides with baking paper, extending paper 5cm over edges.

2 Combine butter and 200g of the chocolate in medium saucepan; stir over low heat until smooth. Cool 10 minutes.

3 Stir sugar, eggs, sifted flours, raspberries and remaining chopped chocolate into chocolate mixture; spread into pan. Bake about 45 minutes. Cool brownie in pan before cutting into 16 slices.

4 Serve brownies dusted with sifted cocoa.

prep + cook time 1 hour 10 minutes **makes** 16

If using frozen raspberries don't thaw them before adding to the mixture otherwise they'll bleed and won't retain their shape.

dutch ginger biscuits

250g butter, softened
¾ cup (165g) firmly packed brown sugar
1 egg
2 cups (300g) plain flour
1 teaspoon ground ginger
⅓ cup (60g) finely chopped glacé ginger

1   Preheat oven to 180°C/160°C fan-forced. Grease oven trays; line with baking paper.
2   Beat butter, sugar and egg in small bowl with electric mixer until combined. Stir in sifted flour and ground ginger, in two batches. Stir in glacé ginger.
3   Roll level tablespoons of dough into balls; place about 3cm apart on trays, flatten with fork. Bake biscuits about 15 minutes; cool on trays.
prep + cook time 35 minutes **makes** 36

pecan choc-chunk cookies

125g butter, softened

¼ cup (55g) caster sugar

¼ cup (55g) firmly packed brown sugar

1 egg

1 cup (150g) plain flour

¾ cup (90g) pecan meal (*see tip, below*)

150g milk eating chocolate, chopped coarsely

½ cup (60g) coarsely chopped pecans

1 Preheat oven to 180°C/160°C fan-forced. Grease oven trays; line with baking paper.

2 Beat butter, sugars and egg in small bowl with electric mixer until combined; stir in sifted flour, meal, chocolate and nuts.

3 Drop level tablespoons of mixture about 5cm apart on trays; flatten slightly. Bake about 15 minutes; cool on trays.

prep + cook time 30 minutes **makes** 28

tip You will need to process approximately 1 cup (120g) pecans to get enough pecan meal for this recipe.

fruit mince slice

¾ cup (110g) plain flour
½ cup (75g) self-raising flour
2 tablespoons caster sugar
100g cold butter, chopped coarsely
1 egg yolk
1 tablespoon milk
410g jar fruit mince
2 large apples (400g), peeled, grated coarsely
1 sheet puff pastry
1 egg yolk, extra

1 Grease 19cm x 30cm lamington pan; line base and long sides with baking paper, extending paper 5cm over sides.

2 Sift flours and sugar into large bowl; rub in butter then stir in egg yolk and milk. Turn dough onto floured surface, knead gently until smooth. Cover; refrigerate 30 minutes.

3 Preheat oven to 200°C/180°C fan-forced.

4 Roll dough between sheets of baking paper until large enough to cover base of pan; press into pan. Spread combined fruit mince and apple over dough.

5 Cut pastry into 2cm-wide strips; place strips over filling in a lattice pattern. Brush pastry with a little extra egg yolk; bake slice about 30 minutes. Cool in pan before cutting.

prep + cook time 1 hour (+ refrigeration)
makes 18

rhubarb custard tea cake

200g butter, softened
½ cup (110g) caster sugar
2 eggs
1¼ cups (185g) self-raising flour
⅓ cup (40g) custard powder
4 fresh rhubarb stalks (300g), sliced lengthways
   then cut into 10cm lengths
20g butter, melted
2 teaspoons caster sugar, extra
CUSTARD
2 tablespoons custard powder
¼ cup (55g) caster sugar
1 cup (250ml) milk
20g butter
2 teaspoons vanilla extract

1   Make custard.
2   Preheat oven to 180°C/160°C fan-forced.
Grease deep 20cm-round cake pan; line base
with baking paper.

3   Beat softened butter and sugar in small bowl
with electric mixer until light and fluffy. Beat in
eggs, one at a time. Transfer to medium bowl; stir
in sifted flour and custard powder.
4   Spread half the mixture into pan; spread over
custard. Dollop small spoonfuls of remaining cake
mixture over custard; carefully spread with spatula
to completely cover custard. Top cake mixture with
rhubarb; brush gently with melted butter then
sprinkle with extra sugar.
5   Bake cake about 1¼ hours; cool in pan.
custard   Combine custard powder and sugar in
small saucepan; gradually stir in milk. Cook, stirring,
until mixture boils and thickens slightly. Remove
from heat; stir in butter and extract. Press plastic
wrap over surface of custard to prevent a skin
forming; cool. Whisk until smooth before using.
prep + cook time 1 hour 50 minutes (+ cooling)
serves 8

chocolate velvet cake

125g butter, softened

1 cup (220g) firmly packed brown sugar

½ cup (110g) caster sugar

3 eggs

2 cups (300g) plain flour

⅓ cup (35g) cocoa powder

1 teaspoon bicarbonate of soda

⅔ cup (160g) sour cream

½ cup (125ml) water

CHOCOLATE GLAZE

100g dark eating chocolate, chopped coarsely

60g butter, chopped coarsely

½ cup (80g) icing sugar

¼ cup (60g) sour cream

1   Preheat oven to 180°C/160°C fan-forced. Grease deep 22cm x 32cm rectangular cake pan; line base and sides with baking paper, extending paper 5cm over sides.

2   Place ingredients in large bowl; beat with electric mixer on low speed until ingredients are combined. Increase speed to medium; beat about 3 minutes or until mixture is smooth and pale in colour. Spread mixture into pan.

3   Bake cake about 45 minutes. Stand cake in pan 10 minutes before turning, top-side up, onto wire rack to cool.

4   Meanwhile, make chocolate glaze. Spread cold cake with chocolate glaze. Serve with whipped cream, if you like.

chocolate glaze Stir ingredients in small saucepan over low heat until smooth. Cook, stirring, 2 minutes. Transfer to small bowl; cool 10 minutes. Refrigerate about 20 minutes or until glaze is spreadable.

prep + cook time 1 hour 10 minutes (+ refrigeration) **serves** 16

banana cupcakes with maple cream frosting

60g butter, softened

60g soft cream cheese

¾ cup (165g) firmly packed brown sugar

2 eggs

½ cup (125ml) milk

2 tablespoons maple syrup

1½ cups (225g) self-raising flour

½ teaspoon bicarbonate of soda

2 medium bananas (400g), halved lengthways,
   sliced thinly

MAPLE CREAM FROSTING

30g butter, softened

80g soft cream cheese

2 tablespoons maple syrup

1½ cups (240g) icing sugar

1 Preheat oven to 180°C/160°C fan-forced. Line 12-hole (⅓-cup/80ml) muffin pan with paper cases.

2 Beat butter, cream cheese and sugar in medium bowl with electric mixer until light and fluffy. Beat in eggs, one at a time. Stir in milk, syrup and sifted dry ingredients; fold in bananas.

3 Drop ¼ cups of mixture into each paper case; bake about 30 minutes. Stand cakes in pans 5 minutes before turning, top-side up, onto wire rack to cool.

4 Meanwhile, make maple cream frosting. Spread cakes with frosting.

maple cream frosting Beat butter, cream cheese and syrup in small bowl with electric mixer until light and fluffy; beat in sifted icing sugar, in two batches, until combined.

prep + cook time 40 minutes **makes** 12

allergy-free choc-hazelnut slice

This recipe is gluten-free, yeast-free and wheat-free.

100g dairy-free spread
½ cup (110g) firmly packed brown sugar
2 eggs
¼ cup (60ml) milk
¾ cup (75g) hazelnut meal
¾ cup (100g) gluten-free self-raising flour
2 tablespoons cocoa powder

FUDGE FROSTING
¼ cup (55g) caster sugar
50g dairy-free spread
2 tablespoons water
¾ cup (120g) pure icing sugar
2 tablespoons cocoa powder

1 Preheat oven to 180°C/160°C fan-forced. Grease shallow 22cm-square cake pan; line base and sides with baking paper, extending paper 5cm over edges.

2 Beat spread and sugar in medium bowl with electric mixer until changed to a paler colour. Beat in eggs, one at a time. Stir in milk, meal, sifted flour and cocoa, in two batches.

3 Spread mixture into pan; bake about 20 minutes. Stand cake in pan 10 minutes before turning, top-side up, onto wire rack to cool.

4 Meanwhile, make fudge frosting. Spread cold slice with frosting.

fudge frosting Combine caster sugar, spread and the water in small saucepan; stir over low heat until sugar dissolves. Transfer to medium bowl; gradually stir in sifted icing sugar and cocoa until smooth. Cover; refrigerate 20 minutes. Beat frosting with electric mixer until spreadable.

prep + cook time 40 minutes (+ refrigeration)
serves 25

tip This cake will almost certainly crack, as most ring-shaped cakes do; however, the icing will cover any cracks.

divine ginger cake with caramel icing

¾ cup (165g) firmly packed brown sugar

¾ cup (110g) plain flour

½ cup (75g) self-raising flour

½ teaspoon bicarbonate of soda

2 teaspoons ground ginger

1 teaspoon ground cinnamon

½ teaspoon ground nutmeg

125g butter, softened

2 eggs

⅔ cup (160ml) buttermilk

CARAMEL ICING

60g butter

½ cup (110g) firmly packed brown sugar

2 tablespoons milk

¾ cup (120g) icing sugar

1 Preheat oven to 170°C/150°C fan-forced. Grease deep 20cm ring pan.

2 Sift dry ingredients into medium bowl. Add remaining ingredients; beat with electric mixer on low speed until ingredients are combined. Increase speed to medium; beat about 2 minutes or until mixture is smooth and paler in colour.

3 Pour mixture into pan; bake about 35 minutes. Stand cake in pan 10 minutes before turning, top-side up, onto wire rack to cool.

4 Meanwhile, make caramel icing. Drizzle warm icing over cake.

caramel icing Stir butter, brown sugar and milk in small saucepan over heat until sugar dissolves; bring to the boil then simmer, stirring, 2 minutes. Remove from heat, stir in sifted icing sugar.

prep + cook time 1 hour 5 minutes **serves** 10

This spicy ginger cake with its buttery caramel icing is lovely served as a dessert with vanilla ice-cream.

chocolate beetroot cake

3 small fresh beetroot (300g), peeled
250g butter, softened
1 cup (220g) firmly packed brown sugar
4 eggs
1⅓ cups (250g) dark Choc Bits
1 cup (150g) plain flour
1 cup (150g) self-raising flour
CHOCOLATE GANACHE
100g dark eating chocolate, chopped coarsely
⅓ cup (80ml) cream

1 Preheat oven to 170°C/150°C fan-forced. Grease 12cm x 22cm loaf pan; line base and long sides with baking paper, extending paper over sides.
2 Grate beetroot coarsely.
3 Beat butter and sugar in small bowl with electric mixer until light and fluffy. Beat in eggs, one at a time (mixture might curdle at this stage, but will come together later).
4 Transfer mixture to large bowl, stir in Choc Bits and sifted flours in two batches, then beetroot.
5 Spread mixture into pan; bake about 1½ hours. Stand cake 5 minutes before turning, top-side up, onto wire rack to cool.
6 Meanwhile, make chocolate ganache. Spread cake with ganache.
chocolate ganache Stir ingredients in small saucepan over low heat until smooth; transfer to small bowl. Cover; refrigerate about 40 minutes or until ganache is spreadable. Beat ganache with electric mixer until fluffy and paler in colour.
prep + cook time 2 hours (+ refrigeration)
serves 12

tips Wear disposable gloves when peeling and grating beetroot, as it will stain your skin. Cake can be stored, in the fridge, in an airtight container, for a week, or can be frozen for two months.

chocolate caramel slice

¾ cup (110g) plain flour

⅓ cup (25g) desiccated coconut

⅓ cup (75g) firmly packed brown sugar

90g butter, melted

395g can sweetened condensed milk

60g butter, extra

2 tablespoons maple syrup

200g dark eating chocolate, chopped coarsely

2 teaspoons vegetable oil

1 Preheat oven to 170°C/150°C fan-forced. Grease shallow 22cm-square cake pan; line base and sides with baking paper, extending paper 5cm above edges.

2 Combine sifted flour, coconut, sugar and butter in medium bowl; press mixture firmly over base of pan. Bake about 15 minutes or until browned lightly; cool.

3 Meanwhile, combine condensed milk, extra butter and syrup in small saucepan; stir over medium heat until smooth, pour over base. Return to oven; bake 25 minutes. Cool.

4 Combine chocolate and oil in small saucepan; stir over low heat until smooth. Pour chocolate over caramel. Refrigerate slice about 3 hours or until set before cutting.

prep + cook time 45 minutes (+ refrigeration)

serves 16

Baking for kids' lunchboxes

Slices, cupcakes, fruit bread, quiches, scrolls

vegemite cheese straws

2 sheets puff pastry
1 tablespoon Vegemite
⅔ cup (50g) finely grated parmesan cheese

1   Preheat oven to 220°C/200°C fan-forced. Oil oven trays; line with baking paper.
2   Spread one pastry sheet with half the Vegemite; sprinkle with half the cheese. Top with remaining pastry sheet; spread with remaining Vegemite, then sprinkle with remaining cheese.
3   Cut pastry stack in half; place one stack on top of the other, press down firmly. Cut pastry crossways into 24 strips; twist each strip, pinching ends to seal. Place on trays; bake about 12 minutes or until browned lightly.
prep + cook time 30 minutes   **makes** 24

spinach and fetta pinwheels

250g frozen spinach, thawed
100g fetta cheese, crumbled
½ cup (40g) finely grated parmesan cheese
2 sheets puff pastry
1 egg

1 Preheat oven to 220°C/200°C fan-forced. Oil oven trays; line with baking paper.

2 Squeeze excess moisture from spinach. Chop spinach coarsely; pat dry between sheets of absorbent paper.

3 Sprinkle spinach and combined cheeses over pastry sheets. Roll pastry tightly to enclose filling. Cut each roll into 12 slices.

4 Place pinwheels, cut-side up, on trays; brush with a little egg. Bake about 15 minutes or until browned lightly.

prep + cook time 30 minutes **makes** 24

sun-dried tomato and bacon scrolls

2 cups (300g) self-raising flour
1 tablespoon caster sugar
50g cold butter, chopped coarsely
¾ cup (180ml) milk
¼ cup (65g) sun-dried tomato pesto
1 cup (120g) pizza cheese
3 rindless bacon rashers (210g), chopped finely
2 tablespoons finely chopped fresh chives

1 Preheat oven to 200°C/180°C fan-forced. Oil shallow 22cm-square cake pan.
2 Sift flour and sugar into medium bowl; rub in butter. Add milk; mix to a soft, sticky dough. Turn dough onto floured surface; knead lightly until smooth. Roll dough into a 30cm x 40cm rectangle.
3 Spread dough with pesto; sprinkle with combined cheese, bacon and chives. Roll dough tightly from long side. Using serrated knife, trim ends. Cut roll into 12 slices; place scrolls, cut-side up, in pan. Bake about 25 minutes.
prep + cook time 40 minutes **makes** 12

pumpkin and corn roll

You need to cook about 400g pumpkin to make enough mashed pumpkin for this recipe.

90g butter, softened
⅓ cup (75g) firmly packed brown sugar
1 egg
125g can corn kernels, rinsed, drained
½ cup (125g) cold mashed pumpkin
1 cup (160g) wholemeal self-raising flour
2 tablespoons milk

note The tin needs to be coated thickly with melted butter so the roll won't stick to the inside of the tin. Don't use cooking-oil spray, as this doesn't give a good enough coating and the roll will stick and be hard to turn out.

1 Adjust oven shelves to fit upright nut roll tins. Preheat oven to 170°C/150°C fan-forced. Grease lids and inside of 8cm x 20cm nut roll tin evenly with melted butter; place base lid on tin, position tin upright on oven tray.

2 Beat butter and sugar in small bowl with electric mixer until light and fluffy. Beat in egg then stir in remaining ingredients. Spoon mixture into tin; tap tin firmly on bench to remove any air pockets; position top lid.

3 Bake roll about 1 hour. Stand loaf in tin 5 minutes; remove lids, shake tin gently to release loaf onto wire rack to cool.

prep + cook time 1 hour 15 minutes
(+ cooling) **serves** 10

tips If you can't find nut roll tins, this mixture can be baked – at the same temperature as above – in a greased and lined 15cm x 25cm loaf pan for about 1¼ hours. Spoon the mixture into the loaf pan, cover pan with a strip of pleated foil (the pleat allows the loaf to rise evenly), and bake for 1 hour, then remove the foil and bake about a further 15 minutes. Baking the loaf this way will make the texture of the loaf similar to the loaves baked in nut roll tins. If you like, you can try making your own nut roll tins out of tall fruit juice cans; see the tip on page 49 for details.

fetta and prosciutto quiches

6 slices (150g) mountain bread
6 eggs
½ cup (125ml) milk
100g fetta cheese, crumbled
100g prosciutto, chopped coarsely
2 green onions, sliced thinly

1 Preheat oven to 170°C/150°C fan-forced. Oil six-hole (¾-cup/180ml) texas muffin pan.
2 Cut a 17.5cm round from each slice of bread. Gently press rounds into pan holes to make cups.
3 Whisk eggs and milk in large jug; stir in remaining ingredients. Pour egg mixture into bread cups; bake about 45 minutes or until set.
4 Stand quiches in pan 5 minutes. Loosen quiches from edges of pan before lifting onto wire rack to cool.
prep + cook time 1 hour **makes 6**

tip A saucer is a good substitute for the cutter.

carrot and zucchini muffins

2 cups (300g) self-raising flour

½ cup (110g) firmly packed brown sugar

1 teaspoon ground cumin

½ teaspoon bicarbonate of soda

1 cup (110g) lightly packed,
   coarsely grated carrot

1 cup (110g) lightly packed,
   coarsely grated zucchini

½ cup (60g) coarsely grated
   cheddar cheese

2 eggs

¾ cup (180ml) buttermilk

90g butter, melted

1   Preheat oven to 200°C/180°C fan-forced. Line 12-hole (⅓-cup/80ml) muffin pan with paper cases.

2   Sift flour, sugar, cumin and soda into large bowl; stir in carrot, zucchini and cheese then eggs, buttermilk and butter. Do not over-mix; mixture should be lumpy.

3   Drop ¼ cups of mixture into paper cases; bake about 20 minutes. Stand muffins in pan 5 minutes before turning, top-side up, onto wire rack to cool.

prep + cook time 30 minutes **makes** 12

note You need two medium carrots (240g) and two small zucchini (180g) for this recipe.

apple raspberry bread

375ml jar apple sauce

1 cup (220g) firmly packed dark brown sugar

2 eggs

40g butter, melted

½ cup (125ml) buttermilk

¼ cup (90g) honey

1½ cups (225g) plain flour

⅔ cup (100g) wholemeal self-raising flour

½ teaspoon bicarbonate of soda

250g fresh or frozen raspberries

1 Preheat oven to 170°C/150°C fan-forced. Grease 12cm x 22cm loaf pan; line base and long sides with baking paper, extending paper 5cm over sides.

2 Combine apple sauce, sugar, eggs, butter, buttermilk and honey in large bowl; stir in sifted dry ingredients. Do not over-mix; mixture should be lumpy. Fold in raspberries.

3 Spread mixture into pan; bake about 1 hour 40 minutes. Stand bread in pan 10 minutes before turning, top-side up, onto wire rack to cool.

prep + cook time 1 hour 55 minutes **serves** 12

tips We used a chunky-style apple sauce for this recipe. If using frozen raspberries, use them straight from the freezer as thawed berries will bleed colour through the cake mix. This cake will almost certainly crack, as most loaf-shaped cakes do.

butterscotch peanut slice

150g butter, chopped coarsely

¾ cup (165g) firmly packed brown sugar

¼ cup (60ml) cream

1 cup (150g) plain flour

⅓ cup (50g) self-raising flour

2 eggs

¼ cup (35g) coarsely chopped roasted
   unsalted peanuts

BUTTERSCOTCH ICING

30g butter

¼ cup (55g) brown sugar

1 tablespoon milk

½ cup (80g) icing sugar

1   Preheat oven to 170°C/150°C fan-forced. Grease
shallow 22cm-square cake pan; line base and sides
with baking paper, extending paper 5cm over edges.

2   Combine butter, sugar and cream in medium
saucepan, stir over heat until sugar dissolves;
bring to the boil. Reduce heat; simmer, uncovered,
2 minutes. Cool 10 minutes.

3   Stir sifted flours, eggs and nuts into butter
mixture; spread mixture into pan. Bake about
25 minutes. Stand slice in pan 5 minutes before
turning, top-side up, onto wire rack to cool.

4   Meanwhile, make butterscotch icing. Spread
slice with icing, leave to set before cutting.

butterscotch icing Stir butter, sugar and milk
in small saucepan over low heat until smooth;
bring to the boil. Remove from heat, stir in
sifted icing sugar.

prep + cook time 35 minutes **makes** 16

carrot and orange cupcakes

You need about two medium carrots (240g) to get the amount of grated carrot required for this recipe.

⅔ cup (160ml) vegetable oil

¾ cup (165g) firmly packed brown sugar

2 eggs

1 teaspoon finely grated orange rind

1½ cups (210g) firmly packed coarsely
   grated carrot

1¾ cups (260g) self-raising flour

¼ teaspoon bicarbonate of soda

1 teaspoon mixed spice

ORANGE GLACÉ ICING

2 cups (320g) icing sugar

20g butter, melted

2 tablespoons orange juice, approximately

1 Preheat oven to 180°C/160°C fan-forced. Line 12-hole (⅓-cup/80ml) muffin pan with paper cases.

2 Beat oil, sugar, eggs and rind in small bowl with electric mixer until thick and creamy. Transfer mixture to large bowl; stir in carrot, then sifted dry ingredients.

3 Divide mixture into paper cases; bake about 30 minutes. Stand cakes in pan 5 minutes before turning, top-side up, onto wire rack to cool.

4 Meanwhile, make orange glacé icing. Spread cakes with icing.

orange glacé icing Sift icing sugar into small heatproof bowl; stir in butter and enough juice to make a firm paste. Stir over small saucepan of simmering water until spreadable.

prep + cook time 50 minutes **makes** 12

Oranges and carrots are a great combination, and the orange icing gives just the right finish to these delicious little cupcakes.

chocolate sticky date cakes

1¾ cups (250g) seeded dried dates
1⅓ cups (330ml) boiling water
1 teaspoon bicarbonate of soda
125g butter, softened
¾ cup (165g) firmly packed brown sugar
3 eggs
1½ cups (225g) self-raising flour
½ cup (95g) dark Choc Bits
CHOCOLATE ICING
1½ cups (240g) icing sugar
1 tablespoon cocoa powder
50g butter, melted
2 tablespoons hot water, approximately

1 Preheat oven to 180°C/160°C fan-forced. Grease 16 holes of two 12-hole (⅓-cup/80ml) muffin pans.

2 Combine dates and the water in small saucepan; bring to the boil. Remove from heat; stir in soda, stand 10 minutes. Blend or process mixture until almost smooth. Cool 10 minutes.

3 Beat butter and sugar in small bowl with electric mixer until light and fluffy. Beat in eggs, one at a time. Transfer mixture to large bowl; stir in sifted flour, chocolate and date mixture.

4 Divide mixture into pan holes; bake about 25 minutes. Stand cakes in pan 10 minutes before turning, top-side up, onto wire rack to cool.

5 Meanwhile, make chocolate icing. Spread cakes with icing.

chocolate icing Sift icing sugar and cocoa into small bowl; stir in butter and enough hot water to make icing spreadable.

prep + cook time 45 minutes **makes** 16

raisin and honey oat bread

1¾ cups (260g) self-raising flour

½ cup (110g) firmly packed brown sugar

⅔ cup (60g) rolled oats

1 cup (180g) raisins

2 eggs

½ cup (125ml) buttermilk

½ cup (125ml) vegetable oil

¼ cup (90g) honey

1 Preheat oven to 180°C/160°C fan-forced. Grease 12cm x 22cm loaf pan; line base and long sides with baking paper, extending paper 5cm over sides.

2 Sift flour into large bowl; stir in sugar, oats and raisins. Add eggs, buttermilk, oil and honey; stir to combine.

3 Spread mixture into pan; bake about 1 hour. Stand loaf in pan 10 minutes before turning, top-side up, onto wire rack to cool.

prep + cook time 1 hour 15 minutes **serves** 10

note The bread will almost certainly crack; it doesn't matter, as most goodies baked in loaf pans will crack.

raspberry and apple cupcakes

125g butter, softened

1 teaspoon vanilla extract

¾ cup (165g) caster sugar

2 eggs

1½ cups (225g) self-raising flour

½ cup (125ml) milk

150g fresh or frozen raspberries

1 large apple (200g), peeled, chopped finely

2 teaspoons icing sugar

1 Preheat oven to 180°C/160°C fan-forced. Line 12-hole (⅓-cup/80ml) muffin pan with paper cases.

2 Beat butter, extract and sugar in small bowl with electric mixer until light and fluffy. Beat in eggs, one at a time. Stir in sifted flour and milk, in two batches. Stir in raspberries and apple.

3 Divide mixture into paper cases; bake about 30 minutes. Stand cakes in pan 5 minutes before turning, top-side up, onto wire rack to cool. Dust with sifted icing sugar.

prep + cook time 45 minutes **makes** 12

tip If using frozen raspberries, use them straight from the freezer as thawed berries will bleed colour through the cake mix.

banana loaves with muesli topping

You need one large overripe banana (230g) to get the amount of mashed banana needed for this recipe.

75g butter, softened
⅓ cup (75g) firmly packed brown sugar
1 egg
¾ cup (110g) self-raising flour
¼ teaspoon bicarbonate of soda
½ cup (115g) mashed overripe banana
¼ cup (60g) sour cream
1 tablespoon milk
¾ cup (75g) untoasted muesli
¼ cup (35g) dried cranberries

1 Preheat oven to 180°C/160°C fan-forced. Grease six holes of 8-hole (¾-cup/180ml) petite loaf pan.
2 Beat butter and sugar in small bowl with electric mixer until light and fluffy. Beat in egg. Stir in sifted dry ingredients, banana, sour cream and milk.
3 Divide mixture into prepared pan holes; sprinkle with combined muesli and cranberries. Bake about 25 minutes. Stand loaves in pan 5 minutes before turning, top-side up, onto wire rack to cool.
prep + cook time 45 minutes **makes 6**

muesli slice

125g butter, chopped coarsely

⅓ cup (75g) firmly packed brown sugar

2 tablespoons honey

1⅓ cups (120g) rolled oats

½ cup (40g) shredded coconut

½ cup (75g) self-raising flour

½ cup (65g) dried cranberries

½ cup (80g) finely chopped dried pineapple

½ cup (70g) slivered almonds

2 tablespoons pepitas

1 Preheat oven to 180°C/160°C fan-forced. Grease 19cm x 30cm lamington pan; line base and long sides with baking paper, extending paper 5cm over sides.

2 Heat butter, sugar and honey in medium saucepan; stir until sugar dissolves. Stir in remaining ingredients.

3 Press mixture firmly into pan; bake about 20 minutes. Cool in pan before cutting.

prep + cook time 40 minutes **makes** 30

note Pepitas are also known as dried pumpkin seeds; they are available from health-food stores and most supermarkets.

fruity popcorn macaroons

3 egg whites
¾ cup (165g) caster sugar
½ cup (40g) desiccated coconut
2 tablespoons plain flour
2 cups (20g) air-popped popcorn
½ cup (80g) finely chopped dried apricots

1 Preheat oven to 150°C/130°C fan-forced. Grease oven trays; line with baking paper.

2 Beat egg whites in small bowl with electric mixer until soft peaks form. Gradually add sugar, beating until sugar dissolves. Transfer to large bowl; fold in coconut and sifted flour, then popcorn and apricots.

3 Drop heaped tablespoons of mixture about 5cm apart onto trays; bake about 20 minutes. Cool on trays.

prep + cook time 35 minutes **makes** 24

tip You need unflavoured, unsalted popcorn for this recipe. If you can't find it, you need to pop 2 tablespoons of popping corn to get 2 cups. Put the corn into a large saucepan with a tight-fitting lid. Put the pan over a medium heat and wait until you hear the popping. Carefully shake the pan over the heat – wait until the popping stops completely then remove the pan from the heat. Wait a minute or two before removing the lid.

Baking for morning tea

Cakes, friands, scones, biscuits, pies, tarts, frittatas, muffins

cream cheese fruit cake

100g soft cream cheese

50g butter, softened

½ cup (110g) caster sugar

2 tablespoons golden syrup

2 teaspoons finely grated orange rind

2 eggs

1 cup (110g) coarsely grated carrot

¾ cup (180g) chopped mixed glacé fruit

⅔ cup (100g) plain flour

⅔ cup (100g) self-raising flour

⅓ cup (80ml) orange juice

1   Preheat oven to 180°C/160°C fan-forced. Grease deep 20cm ring pan.

2   Beat cream cheese, butter, sugar, syrup and rind in large bowl with electric mixer until light and fluffy. Beat in eggs, one at a time. Stir in carrot, fruit, sifted flours and juice. Spread mixture into pan.

3   Bake about 50 minutes. Stand cake 15 minutes before turning, top-side up, onto wire rack to cool.

prep + cook time 1 hour 10 minutes **serves** 10

note We used glacé peaches and pineapple in this recipe. Glacé pears, apricots, cherries and figs could also be used.

note Ring-shaped cakes generally crack because of the confined area in the tin; it doesn't matter – the cake will still taste great.

lemon curd friands

6 egg whites
185g butter, melted
1 cup (120g) almond meal
1½ cups (240g) icing sugar
½ cup (75g) plain flour
¼ cup (80g) lemon curd

1 Preheat oven to 200°C/180°C fan-forced.
Grease 12-hole (½-cup/125ml) oval friand pan.
2 Place egg whites in medium bowl; whisk lightly
with fork until combined. Stir in butter, meal,
sifted icing sugar and flour only until combined.
3 Divide mixture among pan holes; bake
10 minutes. Remove friands from oven; top each
with a level teaspoon of curd. Bake a further
10 minutes. Stand friands 5 minutes before
turning, top-side up, onto wire rack to cool.
prep + cook time 35 minutes **makes** 12

lemon currant loaf

125g butter, softened
1 cup (220g) caster sugar
2 teaspoons finely grated lemon rind
3 eggs
1 cup (150g) self-raising flour
½ cup (75g) plain flour
⅓ cup (80g) sour cream
2 tablespoons lemon juice
1 cup (160g) dried currants

1   Preheat oven to 180°C/160°C fan-forced. Grease 12cm x 22cm loaf pan; line base and long sides with baking paper, extending paper 5cm over sides.
2   Beat butter, sugar and rind in medium bowl with electric mixer until light and fluffy. Beat in eggs, one at a time. Stir in sifted flours, sour cream and juice, in two batches. Stir in currants.
3   Spread mixture into pan; bake about 1 hour 10 minutes. Stand loaf in pan 10 minutes before turning, top-side up, onto wire rack to cool.
prep + cook time 1 hour 30 minutes serves 10

note This cake may crack a little, as most loaf-shaped cakes do this.

spiced apple scones

3½ cups (525g) self-raising flour

2 tablespoons icing sugar

1 teaspoon ground nutmeg

1 teaspoon ground cinnamon

60g cold butter, chopped coarsely

⅔ cup (160ml) water

1½ cups (375ml) buttermilk

1 cup (75g) finely chopped dried apple

1 tablespoon milk

GOLDEN SYRUP BUTTER

100g butter, softened

1 tablespoon golden syrup

1 Preheat oven to 220°C/200°C fan-forced. Grease deep 22cm x 32cm rectangular cake pan.

2 Sift flour, icing sugar and spices into large bowl; rub in butter. Add the water, buttermilk and apple to flour mixture. Use knife to cut buttermilk through the mixture to make a soft, sticky dough. Turn dough onto floured surface; knead lightly until smooth.

3 Press dough into an even 2cm thickness. Dip 5cm-round cutter into flour; cut as many rounds as possible from dough. Place scones side by side, just touching, in pan.

4 Gently knead scraps of dough together; repeat pressing and cutting of dough, place in pan. Brush tops with a little milk; bake about 15 minutes.

5 Meanwhile, make golden syrup butter. Serve hot scones with golden syrup butter.

golden syrup butter Whisk ingredients in medium bowl until light and fluffy.

prep + cook time 30 minutes **makes** 20

These scones are at their very best
if made just before serving. Eat
them hot, straight out of the oven.

peanut butter cookies

125g butter, softened
¼ cup (70g) crunchy peanut butter
¾ cup (165g) firmly packed brown sugar
1 egg
1½ cups (225g) plain flour
½ teaspoon bicarbonate of soda
½ cup (70g) roasted unsalted peanuts,
　chopped coarsely

1   Preheat oven to 180°C/160°C fan-forced.
Grease oven trays; line with baking paper.
2   Beat butter, peanut butter, sugar and egg
in small bowl with electric mixer until smooth;
do not over-mix. Transfer mixture to medium
bowl; stir in sifted flour and soda, then nuts.
3   Roll level tablespoons of mixture into balls;
place 5cm apart on trays, flatten with floured
fork. Bake about 12 minutes; cool on trays.
prep + cook time 25 minutes **makes** 30

vanilla bean butter biscuits

125g butter, softened
½ cup (80g) icing sugar
1 vanilla bean
1¼ cups (85g) plain flour

1   Place butter and sifted icing sugar in small
bowl. Split vanilla bean; scrape seeds into bowl.
Beat with electric mixer until light and fluffy;
stir in sifted flour, in two batches.
2   Knead dough on floured surface until smooth.
Shape dough into 25cm-rectangular log. Enclose
log in plastic wrap; refrigerate about 30 minutes
or until firm.
3   Preheat oven to 180°C/160°C fan-forced.
Grease oven trays; line with baking paper.
4   Cut log into 1cm slices; place slices about
2cm apart on trays. Bake about 12 minutes.
Cool on trays.
prep + cook time 30 minutes (+ refrigeration)
makes 22

mini butterfly cakes

45g butter, softened

¼ teaspoon vanilla extract

¼ cup (55g) caster sugar

1 egg

½ cup (75g) self-raising flour

1½ tablespoons milk

⅓ cup (25g) desiccated coconut

⅓ cup (80ml) thickened cream, whipped

CHOCOLATE ICING

½ cup (80g) icing sugar

1 tablespoon cocoa powder

5g softened butter

1 tablespoon milk, approximately

1 Preheat oven to 200°C/180°C fan-forced. Line 18 holes of two 12-hole (1-tablespoon/20ml) mini muffin pans with paper cases.

2 Beat butter, extract, sugar, egg, sifted flour, and milk in small bowl with electric mixer on low speed until ingredients are combined. Increase speed to medium; beat about 2 minutes or until mixture is smooth and paler in colour.

3 Divide mixture into paper cases. Bake about 10 minutes. Stand cakes in pan 5 minutes before turning, top-side up, onto wire rack to cool.

4 Meanwhile, make chocolate icing.

5 Dip cake tops into icing, drain excess icing then dip into coconut. Cut tops from each cake; cut tops in half to make butterfly wings. Spoon cream onto each cake; position wings in cream.

chocolate icing Sift icing sugar and cocoa into medium heatproof bowl; stir in butter and enough of the milk to make a firm paste. Stir over medium saucepan of simmering water until icing is spreadable.

prep + cook time 40 minutes **makes** 18

note The tin needs to be coated thickly with melted butter so the roll won't stick to the inside of the tin. Don't use cooking-oil spray, as this doesn't give a good enough coating and the roll will stick and be hard to turn out.

date and pecan roll

30g butter

½ cup (125ml) boiling water

½ cup (90g) finely chopped dried seeded dates

¼ teaspoon bicarbonate of soda

½ cup (110g) firmly packed brown sugar

1 cup (150g) self-raising flour

¼ cup (30g) coarsely chopped pecans

1 egg

1 Adjust oven shelves to fit upright nut roll tins. Preheat oven to 170°C/150°C fan-forced. Grease lids and inside of 8cm x 20cm nut roll tin evenly with melted butter; place base lid on tin, position tin upright on oven tray.

2 Stir butter and the water in medium saucepan over low heat until butter melts. Remove from heat; stir in dates and soda, then remaining ingredients. Spoon mixture into tin; tap tin firmly on bench to remove air pockets; position top lid.

3 Bake roll about 1 hour. Stand roll 5 minutes; remove lids. Shake gently to release roll onto wire rack. Serve sliced, warm or cold, with butter.

prep + cook time 1 hour 15 minutes **serves** 10

tip Tall 850ml (8cm x 17cm) fruit juice cans make good nut roll tins. Use a can opener that cuts just below the rims to cut one end from the can. Wash and dry the can thoroughly before greasing. Use a double-thickness of foil to cover top of the can and secure with string; slash a hole in the foil top to allow steam to escape during baking.

mini berry pies

300g frozen mixed berries
¼ cup (55g) caster sugar
2 teaspoons cornflour
1 tablespoon water
5 sheets shortcrust pastry
1 egg white
1 tablespoon caster sugar, extra

1 Preheat oven to 200°C/180°C fan-forced.
Grease three 12-hole (1-tablespoon/20ml)
mini muffin pans.
2 Combine berries and sugar in small saucepan;
stir over heat until sugar dissolves. Bring to the
boil. Blend cornflour with the water; stir into
berry mixture. Stir over heat until mixture boils
and thickens. Cool.
3 Cut 36 x 6cm rounds from pastry; press
rounds into pan holes. Cut 36 x 4cm rounds from
remaining pastry. Divide berry mixture among
pastry cases; top with rounds. Press edges firmly
to seal. Brush tops with egg white; sprinkle with
extra sugar. Make small cut in top of each pie.
4 Bake about 20 minutes. Stand pies in pan
10 minutes before turning, top-side up, onto
wire rack. Serve pies warm or cold.
prep + cook time 45 minutes **makes** 36

upside down pear and pistachio cake

¼ cup (35g) coarsely chopped
    unsalted pistachios
1 cup (220g) firmly packed brown sugar
1 large pear (330g), unpeeled, cored,
    sliced thinly
185g butter, softened
3 eggs
¼ cup (35g) plain flour
1¾ cups (210g) almond meal

1 Preheat oven to 200°C/180°C fan-forced. Grease shallow 22cm-round cake pan; line base with baking paper.

2 Combine nuts and 2 tablespoons of the sugar in small bowl; sprinkle over base of pan, top with pear slices.

3 Beat butter and remaining sugar in small bowl with electric mixer until light and fluffy. Beat in eggs, one at a time. Stir in sifted flour and meal.

4 Pour mixture into pan; bake about 35 minutes. Stand cake in pan 10 minutes before turning, top-side down, onto wire rack. Serve cake warm or cold.

prep + cook time 50 minutes **serves** 8

leek and parmesan mini frittatas

10g butter
1 small leek (200g), sliced thinly
3 eggs
½ cup (125ml) cream
½ cup (40g) coarsely grated parmesan cheese
1 teaspoon dijon mustard
¼ cup finely chopped fresh chives

1 Preheat oven to 170°C/150°C fan-forced. Oil 20 holes of 24-hole (1-tablespoon/20ml) silicone mini muffin pan.

2 Melt butter in medium frying pan; cook leek, stirring, about 10 minutes or until leek softens. Cool.

3 Lightly whisk eggs in medium bowl, stir in leek and remaining ingredients; pour mixture into pan holes. Bake about 20 minutes. Stand frittatas in pan 5 minutes before turning, top-side up, onto wire rack to cool.

prep + cook time 35 minutes **makes** 20

hazelnut espresso friands

185g butter
1 tablespoon instant coffee granules
6 egg whites
1 cup (100g) hazelnut meal
1½ cups (240g) icing sugar
½ cup (75g) plain flour

1   Preheat oven to 200°C/180°C fan-forced.
Grease 12-hole (½-cup/125ml) oval friand pan.
2   Melt butter with coffee in small saucepan over
low heat until coffee dissolves; cool 10 minutes.
3   Using fork, whisk egg whites in medium bowl
until combined. Stir in butter mixture, meal,
sifted icing sugar and flour until combined.
4   Drop ¼ cup of mixture into pan holes; bake
about 25 minutes. Stand friands in pan 5 minutes
before turning, top-side up, onto wire rack to cool.
prep + cook time 40 minutes **makes** 12

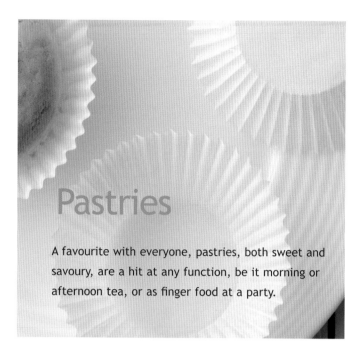

Pastries

A favourite with everyone, pastries, both sweet and savoury, are a hit at any function, be it morning or afternoon tea, or as finger food at a party.

chocolate custard tarts

caprese tartlets

brie and quince matchsticks

brown sugar pecan palmiers

pear frangipane galette

chocolate custard tarts

Preheat oven to 220°C/200°C fan-forced. Grease two 12-hole (1-tablespoon/20ml) mini muffin pans. Combine 3 egg yolks, ½ cup caster sugar, 2 tablespoons cornflour and 1 tablespoon cocoa in medium saucepan; whisk in ¾ cup milk and ⅔ cup cream until smooth. Stir over heat until mixture boils and thickens; cool. Cut 1 sheet puff pastry in half; stack two halves, press firmly. Roll pastry up tightly from long side; cut log into 24 slices. Roll slices between sheets of baking paper into 6cm rounds; press rounds into pan holes. Pour custard into pastry cases; bake about 15 minutes. Cool in tin. Dust with sifted icing sugar, if you like.

prep + cook time 40 minutes **makes** 24

caprese tartlets

Preheat oven to 220°C/200°C fan-forced. Cut nine 7cm rounds from 1 sheet shortcrust pastry. Place rounds on baking-paper-lined oven tray; pierce with fork. Bake about 10 minutes. Spread rounds with 2 tablespoons basil pesto dip. Top rounds with 9 thinly sliced cherry tomatoes and 9 thinly sliced cherry bocconcini cheese. Bake about 2 minutes or until cheese softens. Top each tartlet with a baby basil leaf.

prep + cook time 30 minutes **makes** 9

brie and quince matchsticks

Preheat oven to 220°C/200°C fan-forced. Cut 1 sheet puff pastry into ten 12cm x 4.5cm rectangles. Cut 250g wedge brie cheese into 10 slices. Place pastry rectangles on greased oven tray; pierce with fork. Bake about 10 minutes. Top hot matchsticks with cheese, a lemon thyme sprig and a little quince paste. Serve warm.

prep + cook time 20 minutes **makes** 10

brown sugar pecan palmiers

Preheat oven to 200°C/180°C fan-forced. Process 1 cup pecans, ⅓ cup brown sugar, 50g butter and 1 teaspoon grated orange rind until chopped finely. Sprinkle 1 sheet puff pastry with half the nut mixture; fold two opposite sides of pastry inwards to meet in the centre. Flatten folded edges; brush with a little beaten egg. Fold each side in half again to meet in the centre; flatten slightly and brush with egg. Fold two sides in half again to meet in the centre. Repeat process with another pastry sheet, remaining nut mixture and egg. Enclose each log in plastic wrap; refrigerate 30 minutes. Cut pastry into 1cm slices; place, cut-side up, on baking-paper-lined oven trays. Bake about 15 minutes; cool.

prep + cook time 35 minutes (+ refrigeration) **makes** 48

pear frangipane galette

Preheat oven to 220°C/200°C fan-forced. Beat 40g soft butter, 2 tablespoons caster sugar and 1 egg yolk in small bowl with electric mixer until light and creamy. Stir in ½ cup almond meal and 1 tablespoon plain flour. Cut 1 sheet shortcrust pastry into quarters; place on baking-paper-lined oven tray. Spread almond mixture onto pastry squares, leaving 2cm border. Arrange 1 thinly sliced medium unpeeled corella pear between squares; brush pear with 2 tablespoons warmed, redcurrant jelly. Fold edges of pastry over to form a border; bake about 15 minutes.

prep + cook time 45 minutes **makes** 4

plum jam scone ring

2 cups (300g) self-raising flour

1 tablespoon caster sugar

30g butter, chopped coarsely

¾ cup (180ml) milk

1 egg yolk

¼ cup (80g) plum jam

½ cup (80g) coarsely chopped raisins

1 tablespoon icing sugar

1 Preheat oven to 200°C/180°C fan-forced. Grease oven tray, line with baking paper.

2 Sift flour and sugar into medium bowl; rub in butter. Add combined milk and egg yolk; use a knife to cut milk mixture through flour mixture to make a soft, sticky dough. Turn dough onto floured surface; knead lightly until smooth. Roll dough into 30cm x 40cm rectangle.

3 Spread jam over dough; sprinkle with raisins. Roll dough firmly (but not too tightly) from one long side; place log on tray. Curve log to form a ring; press ends together to seal. Cut around outside of ring at 4cm intervals, cutting all the way down to the tray but not cutting all the way through to the inside of the ring.

4 Bake about 30 minutes. Serve warm dusted with sifted icing sugar.

prep + cook time 45 minutes **serves** 8

This is the epitome of easy baking.
A simple scone mixture filled with
jam and served warm with a cuppa.

cheese scones

1½ cups (225g) self-raising flour
50g butter, chopped coarsely
⅓ cup (40g) coarsely grated cheddar cheese
⅓ cup (25g) coarsely grated parmesan cheese
¼ teaspoon cayenne pepper
¾ cup (180ml) buttermilk

1 Preheat oven to 220°C/200°C fan-forced. Oil shallow 20cm-round cake pan.

2 Sift flour into large bowl; rub in butter. Stir in cheddar cheese, half of the parmesan cheese and the cayenne pepper.

3 Add buttermilk to flour mixture; use a knife to cut buttermilk through the mixture to make a soft, sticky dough. Turn dough onto floured surface; knead lightly until smooth.

4 Press dough into an even 2cm thickness. Dip 5.5cm-round cutter into flour; cut as many rounds as possible from dough. Place scones side by side, just touching, in pan.

5 Gently knead scraps of dough together; repeat pressing and cutting of dough, place in pan. Sprinkle tops with remaining parmesan cheese. Bake about 20 minutes.

prep + cook time 35 minutes **makes** 8

triple choc muffins

1¾ cups (260g) self-raising flour

½ cup (50g) cocoa powder

¾ cup (165g) firmly packed brown sugar

½ cup (95g) dark Choc Bits

½ cup (95g) white Choc Bits

2 eggs

1 cup (250ml) buttermilk

⅔ cup (160ml) vegetable oil

12 white chocolate Melts

1 Preheat oven to 200°C/180°C fan-forced. Line 12-hole (⅓-cup/80ml) muffin pan with paper cases.

2 Sift flour and cocoa into large bowl; stir in sugar and Choc Bits. Stir in combined eggs, buttermilk and oil. Do not over-mix; mixture should be lumpy.

3 Divide mixture into paper cases. Bake muffins 20 minutes; remove from oven. Top each muffin with a chocolate Melt; bake a further 2 minutes.

4 Stand muffins in pan 5 minutes before turning, top-side up, onto wire rack to cool.

prep + cook time 35 minutes **makes** 12

Baking with the kids

Really simple cakes, biscuits, slices & muffins

barbecued chicken pizzas

2 sheets puff pastry

¼ cup (60ml) barbecue sauce

1 cup (160g) shredded barbecued chicken

⅓ cup (80g) drained, coarsely chopped
    roasted red capsicum

1 green onion, sliced thinly

1 cup (100g) pizza cheese

1   Preheat oven to 200°C/180°C fan-forced.
Oil oven trays.

2   Cut eight 11.5cm rounds from pastry;
place on trays.

3   Spread rounds with sauce; top with chicken,
capsicum, onion and cheese. Bake about
15 minutes or until browned.

prep + cook time 30 minutes **makes 8**

bolognese turnovers

2 teaspoons olive oil

1 small brown onion (80g), chopped finely

1 clove garlic, crushed

500g beef mince

2 tablespoons tomato paste

⅔ cup (170g) bottled tomato pasta sauce

⅓ cup finely chopped fresh flat-leaf parsley

4 sheets shortcrust pastry

1 egg, beaten lightly

1 Preheat oven to 200°C/180°C fan-forced. Oil oven trays.

2 Heat oil in large frying pan; cook onion and garlic, stirring, until onion softens. Add beef; cook, stirring, until beef is cooked through. Add paste and sauce; cook, stirring, until heated through. Remove from heat; stir in parsley.

3 Cut sixteen 11.5cm rounds from pastry. Spoon ¼ cup of beef mixture into centre of each round. Brush edges with a little egg; fold rounds in half to enclose filling, pinch edges to seal.

4 Place turnovers on trays; brush with egg. Bake about 15 minutes or until browned.

prep + cook time 45 minutes **makes** 16

kids' cakes

Make one quantity each of the buttercake and butter cream recipes – you will be able to make eight cakes. Decorate them using any of these ideas.

flower pots

froggy

flower power

clown's face

beach babes

buttercake

1 cup (150g) self-raising flour
90g butter, softened
1 teaspoon vanilla extract
½ cup (110g) caster sugar
2 eggs
2 tablespoons milk
BUTTER CREAM
125g butter, softened
1½ cups (240g) icing sugar
2 tablespoons milk

1   Preheat oven to 180°C/160°C fan-forced. Line
eight holes of 12-hole (⅓-cup/80ml) muffin pan with
paper cases
2   Sift flour into small bowl, add remaining ingredients;
beat with electric mixer on low speed until ingredients
are combined. Increase speed to medium; beat until
mixture is smooth and changed to a paler colour.
3   Divide mixture into paper cases. Bake about
20 minutes. Stand cakes in pan 5 minutes before
turning, top-side up, onto wire rack to cool.
4   Meanwhile, make butter cream. Ice cakes
according to directions of chosen cakes.
butter cream   Beat butter in small bowl with electric
mixer until as white as possible; beat in sifted icing
sugar and milk, in two batches.
variation
chocolate butter cream   Sift 2 tablespoons cocoa
powder in with the icing sugar.

flower pots

Smooth a generous amount of chocolate butter cream
over top of cake. Sprinkle with crumbled Flake. Push a
lolly pop into centre of cake; gently push mint leaves
into icing around base of the lollypop.

froggy

Tint butter cream green. Smooth a generous amount
of green butter cream over top of cake. Use scissors
to cut white marshmallow in half crossways. Cut small
piece from base of each marshmallow to give a straight
side. Gently press straight sides into centre of cake,
cut-side facing forward. Press a blue smartie on to
each cut-side of marshmallows.

flower power

Smooth a generous amount of butter cream over top
of cake. Dip cake top into yellow sprinkles. Gently
push white chocolate Melts around edge of cake to
make flower petals.

clown's face

Smooth a generous amount of butter cream over top
of cake. Arrange candy-coloured popcorn for clown's
hair. Use jaffas and red sour strap to make features
on clown's face.

beach babes

Smooth a generous amount of butter cream over top
of cake. Sprinkle with brown sugar. Using a small sharp
knife, thinly slice a small piece from a licorice all-sort
to make beach mat; top with jelly baby. Gently push
paper cocktail umbrella into cake.

choc-chip jaffa muffins

2½ cups (375g) self-raising flour
100g cold butter, chopped finely
1 cup (220g) caster sugar
1¼ cups (310ml) buttermilk
1 egg
¾ cup (135g) dark Choc Bits
2 teaspoons finely grated orange rind

1 Preheat oven to 200°C/180°C fan-forced. Grease 12-hole (⅓-cup/80ml) muffin pan.
2 Sift flour into large bowl; rub in butter. Stir in sugar, buttermilk and egg. Do not over-mix; mixture should be lumpy. Stir in Choc Bits and rind.
3 Divide mixture into pan holes; bake about 20 minutes. Stand muffins in pan 5 minutes before turning, top-side up, onto wire rack to cool.
prep + cook time 30 minutes **makes** 12

3 x 60g Mars Bars

150g butter, chopped coarsely

150g dark eating chocolate, chopped coarsely

½ cup (110g) firmly packed brown sugar

1 cup (250ml) water

½ cup (75g) plain flour

¼ cup (35g) self-raising flour

2 eggs

CHOCOLATE FUDGE FROSTING

50g dark eating chocolate, chopped coarsely

25g butter

1 cup (160g) icing sugar

1 tablespoon cocoa powder

2 tablespoons hot water, approximately

chocolate fudge mud cakes

1 Preheat oven to 180°C/160°C fan-forced. Grease 12-hole (⅓-cup/80ml) muffin pan.

2 Chop two Mars Bars finely; cut remaining bar into 12 slices.

3 Combine butter, chocolate, sugar and the water in medium saucepan; stir over low heat until smooth. Transfer to large bowl; cool 10 minutes. Whisk in sifted flours then eggs and finely chopped Mars Bar.

4 Divide mixture into pan holes; bake about 25 minutes. Stand cakes in pan 5 minutes before turning, top-side up, onto wire rack to cool.

5 Meanwhile, make chocolate fudge frosting. Spread cakes with frosting; top each with a slice of Mars Bar.

chocolate fudge frosting Stir chocolate and butter in small heatproof bowl over small saucepan of simmering water until smooth (do not allow water to touch base of bowl); stir in sifted icing sugar and cocoa. Stir in enough of the hot water until frosting is spreadable.

prep + cook time 45 minutes **makes** 12

candy cupcakes

80g butter, softened

¼ teaspoon vanilla extract

⅓ cup (75g) caster sugar

2 eggs

1 cup (150g) self-raising flour

2 tablespoons milk

2 x 40g jars mini boiled lollies

1 Preheat oven to 180°C/160°C fan-forced. Line 12-hole (2-tablespoons/40ml) deep flat-based patty pan with paper cases.

2 Combine butter, extract, sugar, eggs, sifted flour and milk in small bowl; beat with electric mixer on low speed until ingredients are combined. Increase speed to medium; beat about 2 minutes or until mixture is smooth and paler in colour.

3 Divide mixture into paper cases; bake 15 minutes. Remove cakes from oven; sprinkle lollies over cakes. Bake a further 5 minutes or until lollies melt. Stand cakes in pan 5 minutes before turning, top-side up, onto wire rack to cool.

prep + cook time 35 minutes **makes** 12

raspberry swirl cake

250g butter, softened
1 teaspoon vanilla extract
1¼ cups (275g) caster sugar
3 eggs
2¼ cups (335g) self-raising flour
¾ cup (180ml) milk
150g frozen raspberries, partly thawed
BUTTER FROSTING
100g butter, softened
1 cup (160g) icing sugar
1 tablespoon milk
pink food colouring

1   Preheat oven to 180°C/160°C fan-forced. Grease deep 23cm-round cake pan; line base and side with baking paper.

2   Beat butter, extract and sugar in medium bowl with electric mixer until light and fluffy. Beat in eggs, one at a time. Stir in sifted flour and milk, in two batches.

3   Divide mixture between two small bowls. Lightly crush raspberries in another small bowl with fork; gently stir crushed raspberries into one bowl of cake mixture. Drop alternate spoonfuls of mixtures into pan. Pull skewer back and forth through cake mixture for a marbled effect.

4   Bake cake about 1 hour. Stand cake in pan 5 minutes before turning, top-side up, onto wire rack to cool.

5   Meanwhile, make butter frosting. Spread plain frosting over cake; dollop cake with spoonfuls of pink frosting, swirl frosting for a marbled effect.

butter frosting Beat butter in small bowl with electric mixer until as white as possible; beat in sifted icing sugar and milk, in two batches. Divide frosting between two small bowls; tint one bowl of frosting pink.

prep + cook time 1 hour 30 minutes **serves** 12

chewy chocolate caramel cookies

125g butter, softened
½ cup (110g) caster sugar
1 egg
1 cup (150g) plain flour
2 tablespoons cocoa powder
2 x 60g Chokito bars, chopped finely

1 Preheat oven to 180°C/160°C fan-forced. Grease oven trays; line with baking paper.
2 Beat butter, sugar and egg in small bowl with electric mixer until smooth; do not overbeat. Transfer mixture to medium bowl; stir in sifted flour and cocoa, then chopped chocolate bar.
3 Drop level tablespoons of mixture about 5cm apart onto trays; bake about 15 minutes. Cool cookies on trays.
prep + cook time 25 minutes **makes** 24

note Chokito bars are chocolate-coated caramel fudge bars with crunchy rice crisps. They are available from supermarkets and confectionery stores.

chocolate freckle slice

note Freckles are small chocolate discs covered with hundreds and thousands (nonpareils). They are available from supermarkets and confectionery stores.

185g butter, softened
220g jar chocolate hazelnut spread
⅓ cup (75g) firmly packed brown sugar
1¾ cups (250g) plain flour
200g packet freckles

1 Preheat oven to 160°C/140°C fan-forced.
Grease 19cm x 30cm lamington pan; line base
and long sides with baking paper, extending
paper 5cm over sides.
2 Beat butter, spread and sugar in small bowl
with electric mixer until combined. Stir in sifted
flour, in two batches.
3 Press dough into pan; smooth surface with
spatula. Bake 25 minutes. Remove pan from
oven; working quickly, press freckles firmly
onto slice in rows about 1.5cm apart. Cool
slice in pan; cut when cold.
prep + cook time 45 minutes **makes** 35

pineapple jelly cakes

6 eggs
⅔ cup (150g) caster sugar
⅓ cup (50g) cornflour
½ cup (75g) plain flour
⅓ cup (50g) self-raising flour
80g packet pineapple jelly crystals
1 cup (80g) desiccated coconut
1 cup (75g) shredded coconut
⅔ cup (160ml) thickened cream

1 Preheat oven to 180°C/160°C fan-forced. Grease 19cm x 30cm lamington pan; line base and long sides with baking paper, extending paper 5cm over sides.

2 Beat eggs in large bowl with electric mixer about 10 minutes or until thick and creamy; gradually add sugar, beating until dissolved between additions. Fold in triple-sifted flours. Spread mixture into pan.

3 Bake about 30 minutes. Turn cake immediately onto baking-paper-covered wire rack to cool.

4 Meanwhile, make jelly according to packet instructions; refrigerate until jelly is set to the consistency of unbeaten egg white.

5 Trim and discard edges from cake; cut cake into 20 squares. Dip each square into jelly; toss in combined coconut. Place on tray, refrigerate 30 minutes.

6 Meanwhile, beat cream in small bowl with electric mixer until firm peaks form. Cut cakes in half; sandwich with cream.

prep + cook time 1 hour (+ refrigeration)
makes 20

A simple cake made luscious by dipping into jelly and coconut and filling with whipped cream.

choc peanut butter squares

¾ cup (210g) smooth peanut butter
50g unsalted butter, softened
¼ cup (55g) firmly packed dark brown sugar
1 cup (160g) icing sugar
250g milk eating chocolate, chopped coarsely
¼ cup (35g) roasted crushed peanuts

1 Preheat oven to 180°C/160°C fan-forced. Grease deep 20cm-square loose-based cake pan.
2 Combine peanut butter, butter, brown sugar and sifted icing sugar in medium bowl; press mixture evenly over base of pan. Bake 10 minutes.
3 Meanwhile, combine chocolate and nuts in small saucepan; stir over low heat until chocolate is melted, pour over base. Refrigerate 3 hours or overnight until set.

prep + cook time 25 minutes (+ refrigeration)
makes 36
tip Store squares at room temperature; they taste better this way than if eaten cold from the refrigerator.

banana cake with passionfruit icing

You need 3 large overripe bananas (690g) to get the amount of mashed banana needed for this recipe.

160g butter, softened
¾ cup (165g) firmly packed brown sugar
2 eggs
1½ cups (350g) mashed banana
1 teaspoon bicarbonate of soda
2 tablespoons hot milk
1 cup (150g) plain flour
⅔ cup (100g) self-raising flour

PASSIONFRUIT ICING

1 cup (160g) icing sugar
2 tablespoons passionfruit pulp, approximately

1 Preheat oven to 180°C/160°C. Grease deep 20cm-round cake pan; line base and side with baking paper.

2 Beat butter and sugar in small bowl with electric mixer until light and fluffy. Beat in eggs, one at a time. Transfer mixture to large bowl; stir in banana. Combine soda and milk in small jug; stir into banana mixture. Stir in sifted flours in two batches. Spread mixture into pan.

3 Bake about 45 minutes. Stand cake in pan 5 minutes before turning, top-side up, onto wire rack to cool.

4 Meanwhile, make passionfruit icing. Drizzle cake with icing.

passionfruit icing Sift icing sugar into small bowl; stir in enough of the passionfruit pulp until icing is pourable.

prep + cook time 1 hour 15 minutes **serves** 10

Baking for afternoon tea

Large cakes, small cakes, fruit loaves, biscuits & slices

lime coconut slice

90g butter, softened

½ cup (110g) caster sugar

1 egg

⅓ cup (50g) self-raising flour

¾ cup (110g) plain flour

1 cup (340g) lime marmalade

COCONUT TOPPING

2 eggs

¼ cup (55g) caster sugar

2 cups (150g) shredded coconut

1 cup (80g) desiccated coconut

1 Preheat oven to 180°C/160°C fan-forced. Grease 19cm x 30cm lamington pan; line base and long sides with baking paper, extending paper 5cm over sides.

2 Beat butter, sugar and egg in small bowl with electric mixer until light and fluffy; stir in sifted flours. Press dough into pan; spread with marmalade.

3 Meanwhile, make coconut topping. Sprinkle topping over marmalade. Bake slice about 45 minutes; cool in pan.

coconut topping Whisk eggs and sugar in medium bowl; stir in coconuts.

prep + cook time 1 hour **serves** 20

white chocolate and macadamia slice

125g butter, chopped coarsely

180g white eating chocolate, chopped coarsely

½ cup (110g) caster sugar

2 eggs

1 cup (150g) plain flour

½ cup (75g) self-raising flour

¾ cup (105g) coarsely chopped
   roasted macadamias

¾ cup (135g) white Choc Bits

1 tablespoon icing sugar

1 Preheat oven to 160°C/140°C fan-forced. Grease 19cm x 30cm lamington pan; line base and long sides with baking paper, extending paper 5cm over sides.

2 Combine butter and chocolate in medium saucepan; stir over low heat until smooth. Cool 10 minutes.

3 Stir sugar and eggs, then sifted flours, nuts and Choc Bits into chocolate mixture. Spread mixture into pan. Bake slice, in oven, about 30 minutes. Cool slice in pan. Dust with sifted icing sugar before serving.

prep + cook time 50 minutes **makes** 20

sour cream chocolate cake

tip This cake has a tendency to crack, however, the ganache will cover it, and it'll still taste great.

125g butter, softened

1 cup (220g) firmly packed brown sugar

2 eggs

⅔ cup (160ml) milk

1 cup (240g) sour cream

2 cups (300g) self-raising flour

⅔ cup (70g) cocoa powder

SOUR CREAM GANACHE

⅔ cup (160g) sour cream

200g dark eating chocolate,
   chopped coarsely

1   Preheat oven to 170°C/150°C fan-forced. Grease deep 23cm-round cake pan; line base and side with baking paper.

2   Beat butter and sugar in small bowl with electric mixer until light and fluffy. Beat in eggs, one at a time. Transfer mixture to large bowl; stir in combined milk and sour cream and sifted dry ingredients in two batches.

3   Spread mixture into pan; tap pan on bench to remove any large air pockets. Bake about 50 minutes. Stand cake in pan 5 minutes before turning, top-side up, onto wire rack to cool.

4   Meanwhile, make sour cream ganache. Split cake in half; sandwich with half the ganache. Spread top of cake with remaining ganache.

sour cream ganache   Combine ingredients in small saucepan; stir over low heat until smooth. Cool about 45 minutes or until spreadable.

prep + cook time 1 hour 15 minutes (+ cooling)

serves 10

walnut and prune loaf

100g butter, softened
¾ cup (165g) caster sugar
2 eggs
2 cups (320g) wholemeal self-raising flour
1 cup (280g) yogurt
⅓ cup (80ml) orange juice
1 cup (190g) finely chopped seeded prunes
⅔ cup (80g) finely chopped roasted walnuts

1 Preheat oven to 180°C/160°C fan-forced. Grease 12cm x 22cm loaf pan; line base and long sides with baking paper, extending paper 5cm over sides.
2 Combine butter, sugar, eggs, sifted flour, yogurt and juice in medium bowl; beat on low speed with electric mixer until combined. Stir in prunes and nuts.
3 Spread mixture into pan; bake about 1¼ hours. Stand loaf in pan 10 minutes before turning, top-side up, onto wire rack to cool.
prep + cook time 1 hour 45 minutes **serves** 10

note The loaf will almost certainly crack; it doesn't matter, as most cakes baked in loaf pans will crack.

pineapple coconut slice

185g butter, softened

¾ cup (165g) caster sugar

3 eggs

⅔ cup (50g) desiccated coconut

1¾ cups (260g) self-raising flour

270ml can coconut cream

440g can crushed pineapple, well-drained

⅓ cup (25g) shredded coconut

LIME GLACÉ ICING

1½ cups (240g) icing sugar

20g butter, melted

2 tablespoons lime juice, approximately

1 Preheat oven to 180°C/160°C fan-forced. Grease 22cm x 32cm rectangular cake pan; line base and sides with baking paper, extending paper 5cm over edges.

2 Beat butter and sugar in small bowl with electric mixer until light and fluffy. Beat in eggs, one at a time. Transfer mixture to large bowl; stir in coconut, sifted flour, coconut cream and pineapple, in two batches.

3 Spread mixture into pan; bake 45 minutes. Stand cake in pan 10 minutes before turning, top-side up, onto wire rack to cool.

4 Meanwhile, make lime glacé icing; spread icing over cake, sprinkle with coconut.

lime glacé icing Sift icing sugar into small heatproof bowl; stir in butter and enough of the juice to make a soft paste. Stir over small saucepan of simmering water until icing is spreadable.

prep + cook time 1 hour **serves** 20

cranberry chewies

¾ cup (60g) flaked almonds

3 egg whites

½ cup (110g) caster sugar

1 tablespoon cornflour

1 teaspoon finely grated orange rind

¾ cup (105g) dried cranberries

1 tablespoon icing sugar

1   Preheat oven to 160°C/140°C fan-forced. Grease oven trays; line with baking paper.

2   Dry roast nuts in medium frying pan until browned lightly, remove from pan. Cool.

3   Beat egg whites in small bowl with electric mixer until soft peaks form. Gradually add sugar, beating until sugar dissolves. Transfer to medium bowl; fold in sifted cornflour, rind, cranberries and nuts, in two batches.

4   Drop heaped tablespoons of mixture about 4cm apart onto trays; bake about 30 minutes. Stand on tray 5 minutes before transferring to wire rack to cool. Dust with sifted icing sugar.

prep + cook time 50 minutes **makes** 18

blueberry yogurt loaf

note The loaf will almost certainly crack; it doesn't matter, as most cakes baked in loaf pans will crack.

150g butter, softened
2 teaspoons finely grated lemon rind
1¼ cups (275g) firmly packed brown sugar
2 eggs
1¼ cups (185g) plain flour
½ cup (75g) self-raising flour
⅔ cup (190g) greek-style yogurt
150g frozen blueberries

1 Preheat oven to 170°C/150°C fan-forced.
Grease 12cm x 22cm loaf pan; line base and
long sides with baking paper, extending paper
5cm over sides.
2 Beat butter, rind and sugar in small bowl
with electric mixer until light and fluffy. Beat
in eggs, one at a time. Transfer to large bowl;
stir in sifted flours and yogurt, in two batches.
Fold in blueberries.
3 Spread mixture into pan; bake 1½ hours.
Stand cake in pan 5 minutes before turning,
top-side up, onto wire rack to cool.
prep + cook time 2 hours **serves** 12

choc-vanilla spiral cookies

200g butter, softened
⅔ cup (150g) caster sugar
1 teaspoon vanilla extract
1 egg
2½ cups (375g) plain flour
1 tablespoon cocoa powder

1 Beat butter, sugar, extract and egg in small bowl with electric mixer until light and fluffy. Divide mixture between two medium bowls; stir half the sifted flour into one bowl, mix to form a firm dough. Stir remaining sifted flour and cocoa into second bowl, mix to form a firm dough. Knead each piece of dough, separately, on a floured surface until smooth; cover, refrigerate 30 minutes.
2 Roll vanilla dough between sheets of baking paper into a 25cm x 35cm rectangle; repeat with chocolate dough. Remove top sheets of baking paper from dough. Turn vanilla dough onto chocolate dough, remove top sheet of paper; trim edges. Using bottom sheet of paper as a guide, roll dough stack tightly from long side. Enclose roll in plastic wrap; refrigerate 30 minutes.
3 Preheat oven to 180°C/160°C fan-forced. Grease oven trays; line with baking paper.
4 Remove plastic from roll; cut roll into 1cm slices. Place slices about 2cm apart on trays; bake about 15 minutes. Stand cookies on trays 5 minutes before transferring to wire rack to cool.
prep + cook time 45 minutes (+ refrigeration)
makes 28

cream cheese, coconut and lime cookies

250g butter, softened

90g soft cream cheese

1 tablespoon finely grated lime rind

1 cup (220g) firmly packed brown sugar

2 eggs

1¼ cups (185g) plain flour

1 cup (150g) self-raising flour

½ cup (40g) desiccated coconut

1 Preheat oven to 180°C/160°C fan-forced. Grease oven trays; line with baking paper.

2 Beat butter, cream cheese, rind and sugar in small bowl with electric mixer until light and fluffy. Beat in eggs, one at a time. Transfer mixture to large bowl; stir in sifted flours and coconut, in two batches.

3 Roll level tablespoons of dough into balls, place about 3cm apart on trays; flatten slightly. Bake about 15 minutes; cool on trays.

prep + cook time 40 minutes **makes** 36

Packet cake mixes

No one need ever know that these delicious cakes came from a packet. Jazz them up with a few extras, and everyone will think that you are so creative.

upside-down toffee date and banana cake

orange raspberry loaf

rhubarb almond cakes

sticky banana and date muffins

choc espresso gateau

upside-down toffee date and banana cake

Preheat oven to 170°C/150°C fan-forced. Grease and line deep 20cm-round cake pan. Stir 50g butter and ½ cup brown sugar in small saucepan over low heat until smooth. Spread mixture over base of pan; top with 2 sliced bananas. Combine 340g packet buttercake mix, 2 eggs, 60g soft butter and ¾ cup milk in medium bowl. Beat on low speed with electric mixer until ingredients are combined. Increase speed to medium; beat 3 minutes. Pour mixture over bananas; bake about 50 minutes. Stand cake in pan 5 minutes before turning, top-side down, onto serving plate.

prep + cook time 1 hour 10 minutes **serves** 12

orange raspberry loaf

Preheat oven to 180°C/160°C fan-forced. Grease 12cm x 22cm loaf pan; line base and long sides with baking paper, extending paper 5cm over sides. Combine 310g packet madeira cake mix, 2 eggs, ¾ cup milk and 2 teaspoons grated orange rind in medium bowl. Beat on low speed with electric mixer until ingredients are combined. Increase speed to medium; beat 3 minutes. Stir in 150g frozen raspberries. Pour mixture into pan; bake about 55 minutes. Stand cake in pan 10 minutes before turning, top-side up, onto wire rack to cool.

prep + cook time 1 hour 10 minutes **serves** 10

rhubarb almond cakes

Preheat oven to 180°C/160°C fan-forced. Grease 8-hole (¾-cup/180ml) petite loaf pan well with melted butter. Combine 340g packet vanilla cake mix, 2 eggs, 40g soft butter, ½ cup almond meal and ⅔ cup milk in medium bowl. Beat on low speed with electric mixer until ingredients are combined. Increase speed to medium; beat 3 minutes. Stir in 1 cup finely chopped fresh rhubarb. Divide mixture into pan holes; top each with two 7cm long thin rhubarb stalks. Bake about 30 minutes. Stand cakes 10 minutes before turning, top-side up, onto wire rack to cool.

prep + cook time 40 minutes **makes** 8

sticky banana and date muffins

Preheat oven to 200°C/180°C fan-forced. Grease 12-hole (⅓-cup/80ml) muffin pan. Place 455g packet banana muffin mix in large bowl; stir in 1 cup finely chopped seeded dried dates. Stir in 1⅓-cups water. Divide mixture into pan holes; bake about 20 minutes. Combine ½ cup brown sugar, ½ cup cream and 40g butter in small pan; stir over low heat until smooth. Simmer until sauce thickens slightly. Stand muffins in pan 5 minutes before turning, top-side up, onto wire rack to cool. Serve muffins with sauce.

prep + cook time 40 minutes **makes** 12

choc espresso gateau

Preheat oven to 180°C/160°C fan-forced. Grease and line deep 20cm-round cake pan. Dissolve 1 tablespoon instant coffee granules in 2 tablespoons boiling water; cool. Combine 370g packet chocolate cake mix, 2 eggs, 20g soft butter, ¾ cup water and coffee mixture in medium bowl. Beat on low speed with electric mixer until ingredients are combined. Increase speed to medium; beat 3 minutes. Pour mixture into pan; bake about 45 minutes. Stand cake in pan 10 minutes before turning, top-side up, onto wire rack to cool. Split cake into three. Beat 300ml thickened cream until firm peaks form; stir in 100g grated dark eating chocolate. Sandwich cake layers with chocolate cream.

prep + cook time 1 hour 10 minutes **serves** 12

shortbread bars with nut crumble

250g butter, softened

½ cup (110g) caster sugar

2 cups (300g) plain flour

½ cup (100g) rice flour

NUT CRUMBLE

⅓ cup (50g) plain flour

25g butter, chopped finely

2 tablespoons caster sugar

¼ cup (30g) finely chopped unsalted pistachios

¼ cup (35g) slivered almonds

1 Preheat oven to 160°C/140°C fan-forced. Grease oven trays; line with baking paper.

2 Beat butter and sugar in medium bowl with electric mixer until light and fluffy; stir in sifted flours, in two batches. Knead dough on floured surface until smooth.

3 Divide dough in half; roll each piece between sheets of baking paper to 12cm x 24cm rectangle, place on tray. Refrigerate 30 minutes.

4 Meanwhile, make nut crumble.

5 Cut dough into 3cm x 6cm bars (you will have 32 bars); place on trays. Press crumble mixture onto shortbread; bake about 15 minutes. Cool on trays.

nut crumble Sift flour into medium bowl; rub in butter. Stir in sugar and nuts.

prep + cook time 45 minutes (+ refrigeration)

makes 32

spiced treacle cookies

75g butter, chopped
⅓ cup (120g) treacle
¼ cup (55g) firmly packed brown sugar
¾ cup (110g) plain flour
½ cup (75g) self-raising flour
1 teaspoon ground cinnamon
1 teaspoon mixed spice
¼ cup (30g) finely chopped walnuts
1 tablespoon brown sugar, extra

1 Preheat oven to 160°C/140°C fan-forced.
Grease oven trays; line with baking paper.
2 Combine butter, treacle and sugar in medium
saucepan; stir over low heat until smooth. Cool
5 minutes; stir in sifted flours and spices.
3 Roll rounded teaspoons of mixture into balls,
place about 5cm apart on trays; flatten slightly.
Sprinkle with combined nuts and extra sugar.
Bake about 20 minutes; cool on trays.
prep + cook time 35 minutes **makes** 34

triple chocolate slice

250g plain chocolate biscuits

325g dark eating chocolate, chopped coarsely

200g butter, chopped coarsely

3 eggs

3 egg yolks

⅓ cup (75g) caster sugar

1 tablespoon cocoa powder

1 Preheat oven to 160°C/140°C fan-forced. Grease 19cm x 30cm lamington pan; line base and long sides with baking paper, extending paper 5cm over sides.

2 Place biscuits in a single layer over base of pan, trimming to fit if necessary.

3 Combine chocolate and butter in medium saucepan; stir over low heat until smooth. Remove from heat.

4 Beat eggs, egg yolks and sugar in medium bowl with electric mixer until thick and creamy; beat in warm chocolate mixture.

5 Pour mixture over biscuits. Bake about 25 minutes or until filling is set. Cool 15 minutes then refrigerate 1 hour. Dust slice with sifted cocoa before cutting.

prep + cook time 40 minutes (+ refrigeration)

makes 30

Baking for celebrations

Slices, sponges, fruit & nut cakes, syrup cakes, chocolate cakes

caramel meringue pies

18 (220g) butternut snap biscuits
380g can Caramel Top 'n' Fill
2 egg whites
⅓ cup (50g) caster sugar
2 tablespoons shredded coconut

1 Preheat oven to 160°C/140°C fan-forced. Grease 18 holes of two 12-hole (1½-tablespoons/30ml) shallow round-based patty pans.
2 Place one biscuit over top of each greased pan hole; bake about 4 minutes or until biscuits soften. Using the back of a teaspoon, gently push softened biscuits into pan holes; cool.

3 Increase oven temperature to 240°C/220°C fan-forced.
4 Place caramel in small bowl; whisk until smooth. Spoon caramel into biscuit cases.
5 Beat egg whites in small bowl with electric mixer until soft peaks form; gradually add sugar, beating until sugar dissolves.
6 Spread meringue over caramel; sprinkle with coconut. Bake pies about 3 minutes or until browned lightly.
prep + cook time 30 minutes **makes** 18

These are simplicity itself to make and take no
more than half an hour, but they look so impressive,
people will think you've spent all day on them.

rocky road brownie slice

100g butter, chopped coarsely
200g dark eating chocolate, chopped coarsely
1 cup (220g) firmly packed brown sugar
2 eggs
½ cup (75g) plain flour
⅓ cup (80g) sour cream
200g toasted marshmallows, chopped coarsely
½ cup (70g) roasted slivered almonds
300g white eating chocolate, melted

1 Preheat oven to 180°C/160°C fan-forced.
Grease 19cm x 30cm lamington pan; line base
and long sides with baking paper, extending
paper 5cm over sides.
2 Combine butter and dark chocolate in medium
saucepan; stir over low heat until smooth. Cool
10 minutes.
3 Stir sugar and eggs, then sifted flour and sour
cream into chocolate mixture. Spread mixture
into pan. Bake slice about 35 minutes; cool in pan.
4 Combine marshmallows and nuts in medium
bowl; sprinkle over slice, drizzle with white
chocolate. Refrigerate until set.
prep + cook time 45 minutes (+ refrigeration)
makes 30

choc-cherry cake

370g packet rich chocolate cake mix

1 cup (250ml) vegetable oil

2½ cups (625ml) water

200g dark eating chocolate, melted

1 cup (220g) firmly packed brown sugar

2 eggs

2 cups (300g) plain flour

½ cup (50g) cocoa powder

1 teaspoon bicarbonate of soda

300g frozen cherries, chopped coarsely

CHOCOLATE SATIN ICING

200g dark eating chocolate, chopped coarsely

125g butter, chopped coarsely

⅓ cup (80g) sour cream

1   Preheat oven to 180°C/160°C fan-forced.
Grease 26.5cm x 36.5cm (16-cup/4-litre) baking
dish; line base and long sides with baking paper,
extending paper 5cm over sides.

2   Combine cake mix, oil, the water, chocolate,
sugar, eggs and sifted dry ingredients in large
bowl; beat on low speed with electric mixer until
ingredients are combined. Increase speed to
medium; beat about 3 minutes or until mixture
is smooth and paler in colour. Stir in cherries.
Pour mixture into dish.

3   Bake about 1 hour 20 minutes. Stand cake
in dish 10 minutes before turning, top-side up,
onto wire rack to cool.

4   Meanwhile, make chocolate satin icing. Spread
cake with icing.

chocolate satin icing Stir chocolate and butter
in small saucepan over low heat until smooth; stir
in sour cream. Refrigerate 5 minutes or until icing
is spreadable.

prep + cook time 1 hour 40 minutes **serves** 30

triple choc cheesecake slice

24 (310g) chocolate-chip cookies
½ cup (125ml) thickened cream
250g white eating chocolate, chopped coarsely
500g soft cream cheese
¾ cup (165g) caster sugar
2 eggs
CHOCOLATE GANACHE
200g dark eating chocolate, chopped coarsely
⅓ cup (80ml) cream

1 Preheat oven to 150°C/130°C fan-forced. Grease 19cm x 30cm lamington pan; line base and long sides with baking paper, extending paper 5cm over sides.

2 Place cookies, in single layer, over base of prepared pan; trim to fit, if necessary.

3 Combine cream and chocolate in small saucepan; stir over low heat until smooth. Cool.

4 Beat cream cheese and sugar in medium bowl with electric mixer until smooth. Beat in eggs, one at a time; beat in chocolate mixture.

5 Pour mixture into pan; bake about 35 minutes or until set. Cool in oven with door ajar. Refrigerate 3 hours or overnight.

6 Make chocolate ganache. Spread ganache over cheesecake; refrigerate until set.

7 Remove cheesecake from pan; remove paper from base before cutting.

chocolate ganache Stir ingredients in small pan over low heat until smooth; cool 15 minutes.

prep + cook time 50 minutes
(+ cooling & refrigeration) **makes** 24

flourless chocolate cakes with latte sauce

150g dark eating chocolate, chopped coarsely

150g butter, chopped coarsely

4 eggs, separated

1 cup (220g) firmly packed brown sugar

1¼ cups (150g) almond meal

LATTE SAUCE

180g white eating chocolate, chopped coarsely

½ cup (125ml) cream

2 tablespoons coffee-flavoured liqueur

1 teaspoon instant coffee granules

1   Preheat oven to 180°C/160°C fan-forced. Grease 12-hole (⅓-cup/80ml) muffin pan.

2   Make latte sauce.

3   Combine chocolate and butter in medium saucepan; stir over low heat until smooth. Cool 5 minutes. Stir in egg yolks, sugar and meal. Transfer to large bowl.

4   Beat egg whites in small bowl with electric mixer until soft peaks form; fold into chocolate mixture, in two batches.

5   Divide mixture among pan holes; bake about 25 minutes. Cool cakes in pan 5 minutes before turning, top-side down, onto serving plates. Serve warm cakes drizzled with latte sauce.

latte sauce   Stir ingredients in small saucepan over low heat until smooth. Cool about 30 minutes or until thickened slightly.

prep + cook time 45 minutes (+ cooling)

makes 12

tip You may need to run a spatula carefully around the edges of the cakes to loosen them before turning out of the pan.

raspberry brownie ice-cream cake

1 litre vanilla ice-cream, softened

150g frozen raspberries

125g butter, chopped coarsely

200g dark eating chocolate, chopped coarsely

½ cup (110g) caster sugar

2 eggs

1¼ cups (185g) plain flour

150g milk eating chocolate, chopped coarsely

1 tablespoon icing sugar

1 Line deep 23cm-round cake pan with plastic wrap, extending wrap so it will cover pan. Combine ice-cream and raspberries in medium bowl. Spoon ice-cream into pan; smooth surface. Fold plastic wrap over to enclose. Freeze 3 hours or until firm.

2 Preheat oven to 160°C/140°C fan-forced. Remove ice-cream from pan, still wrapped in plastic; place on tray. Return to freezer.

3 Grease same pan; line base and side with baking paper.

4 Combine butter, dark chocolate and sugar in medium saucepan; stir over low heat until smooth. Cool 10 minutes.

5 Stir in eggs, sifted flour and milk chocolate. Spread mixture into pan. Bake brownie about 30 minutes; cool in pan.

6 Split brownie in half. Sandwich ice-cream cake between brownie slices; serve immediately, dusted with sifted icing sugar. Serve with fresh raspberries, if you like.

prep + cook time 1 hour (+ freezing) **serves** 12

flourless fig, pecan and maple syrup cake

125g butter, softened

½ cup (110g) firmly packed brown sugar

4 eggs, separated

1½ cups (180g) pecan meal (*see tip, below*)

⅓ cup (55g) semolina

¼ cup (60ml) milk

1 cup (200g) finely chopped dried figs

MAPLE SYRUP

½ cup (125ml) maple syrup

⅓ cup (75g) firmly packed brown sugar

½ cup (125ml) water

tips You will need to blend about 2 cups (240g) pecans to get enough pecan meal for this recipe. Semolina is available from health-food stores and supermarkets. It can be replaced with ⅓ cup (50g) plain flour.

1 Preheat oven to 180°C/160°C fan-forced. Grease deep 23cm-round cake pan; line base and side with baking paper.

2 Beat butter and sugar in small bowl with electric mixer until light and fluffy; beat in egg yolks. Transfer mixture to large bowl; stir in meal and semolina, then milk and figs.

3 Beat egg whites in small bowl with electric mixer until soft peaks form; fold into fig mixture, in two batches. Pour mixture into pan; bake about 40 minutes.

4 Meanwhile, make maple syrup.

5 Stand cake in pan 5 minutes before turning, top-side up, onto wire rack set over tray. Pour hot syrup over hot cake. Serve cake warm.

maple syrup Stir ingredients in small saucepan over low heat until sugar dissolves; bring to the boil. Boil, uncovered, about 5 minutes or until thickened slightly.

prep + cook time 1 hour **serves** 12

¼ cup (60ml) dark rum

1 cup (180g) raisins, chopped finely

300g dark eating chocolate, chopped coarsely

150g butter, chopped coarsely

⅔ cup (150g) firmly packed brown sugar

⅔ cup (100g) self-raising flour

2 tablespoons cocoa powder

3 eggs, separated

2 teaspoons cocoa powder, extra

rum and raisin chocolate cake

1 Preheat oven to 180°C/160°C fan-forced. Grease deep 23cm-round cake pan; line base and side with baking paper.

2 Warm rum in small saucepan, add raisins; stand 1 hour.

3 Combine chocolate and butter in small saucepan; stir over low heat until smooth. Transfer to large bowl; cool 5 minutes. Stir in sugar, sifted flour and cocoa, egg yolks and raisin mixture.

4 Beat egg whites in small bowl with electric mixer until soft peaks form; fold into chocolate mixture, in two batches.

5 Pour mixture into pan; bake about 1 hour. Stand cake in pan 15 minutes before turning, top-side up, onto serving plate. Serve cake warm or cold dusted with extra sifted cocoa. Serve cake with whipped cream, if you like.

prep + cook time 1 hour 15 minutes (+ standing) **serves** 12

spiced sponge with pistachio honey cream

4 eggs

¾ cup (165g) firmly packed dark brown sugar

1 cup (150g) wheaten cornflour

1 teaspoon cream of tartar

½ teaspoon bicarbonate of soda

1 teaspoon mixed spice

½ teaspoon ground cardamom

PISTACHIO HONEY CREAM

300ml thickened cream

1 tablespoon honey

¼ cup (30g) finely chopped roasted
   unsalted pistachios

1 Preheat oven to 180°C/160°C fan-forced. Grease two deep 23cm-round cake pans.

2 Beat eggs and sugar in small bowl with electric mixer about 10 minutes or until sugar dissolves and mixture is thick and creamy; transfer to large bowl. Gently fold in triple-sifted dry ingredients.

3 Divide mixture between pans; bake about 18 minutes. Turn sponges, top-side up, onto baking-paper-covered wire rack to cool.

4 Meanwhile, make pistachio honey cream. Sandwich sponges with cream; dust with a little sifted icing sugar.

pistachio honey cream Beat cream and honey in small bowl with electric mixer until soft peaks form; fold in nuts.

prep + cook time 40 minutes **serves** 10

rich fruit cake with stout

500g (3 cups) mixed dried fruit
1⅔ cups (100g) coarsely chopped dried apple
⅔ cup (100g) coarsely chopped dried peaches
½ cup (85g) coarsely chopped dried figs
200g butter, chopped coarsely
¾ cup (165g) firmly packed brown sugar
375ml stout
4 eggs
1½ cups (225g) plain flour
½ cup (75g) self-raising flour
½ teaspoon bicarbonate of soda
1 teaspoon mixed spice
½ cup (60g) pecans

1 Grease deep 23cm-round cake pan; line base and side with three thicknesses of baking paper, extending paper 5cm above edge.
2 Combine fruit, butter, sugar and stout in large saucepan; stir over medium heat until sugar dissolves. Bring fruit mixture to the boil; transfer to large heatproof bowl. Cool.
3 Preheat oven to 150°C/130°C fan-forced.
4 Stir eggs and sifted dry ingredients into fruit mixture. Spread mixture into pan; decorate with nuts. Bake about 2½ hours. Cover hot cake with foil; cool cake in pan overnight.
prep + cook time 2 hours 45 minutes
(+ cooling) **serves** 16

note Stout is a strong, dark beer that originated in Great Britain in the late 1700s. More redolent of hops than other beers, it is made with roasted barley, giving it its characteristic dark colour and bitter-sweet, almost coffee-like flavour. We used Guinness.

orange, almond and pine nut cake

2 medium oranges (480g)

1 teaspoon baking powder

6 eggs

1 cup (220g) caster sugar

2 cups (240g) almond meal

½ cup (75g) plain flour

⅓ cup (50g) pine nuts

1   Place unpeeled whole oranges in medium saucepan, cover with cold water; bring to the boil. Boil, covered, 1½ hours or until oranges are tender; drain. Cool.

2   Preheat oven to 180°C/160°C fan-forced. Grease deep 23cm-round cake pan; line base and side with baking paper.

3   Trim and discard ends from oranges. Halve oranges; discard seeds. Blend or process oranges, including rind, with baking powder until mixture is pulpy.

4   Beat eggs and sugar in medium bowl with electric mixer about 5 minutes or until thick and creamy. Fold in meal, sifted flour and orange pulp.

5   Pour mixture into pan, sprinkle with nuts; bake about 1 hour. Cool cake in pan.

prep + cook time 3 hours (+ cooling) **serves** 16

tip We used a 20cm (9-cup) silicone baba pan; a metal baba pan can also be used.

lime and ricotta syrup cake

200g butter, softened

1 tablespoon finely grated lime rind

1 cup (220g) caster sugar

3 eggs, separated

250g ricotta cheese

½ cup (125ml) milk

1½ cups (225g) self-raising flour

LIME SYRUP

⅓ cup (80ml) lime juice

¼ cup (60ml) water

⅔ cup (150g) caster sugar

1   Preheat oven to 180°C/160°C fan-forced. Grease 20cm baba pan well with melted butter.

2   Beat butter, rind and sugar in small bowl with electric mixer until light and fluffy. Beat in egg yolks, cheese and milk. Transfer to large bowl; stir in sifted flour.

3   Beat egg whites in small bowl with electric mixer until soft peaks form; fold into cheese mixture, in two batches.

4   Spread mixture into pan; bake about 1 hour. Stand cake in pan 5 minutes before turning onto wire rack set over tray.

5   Meanwhile, make lime syrup. Pour hot syrup over hot cake. Serve cake warm, with whipped cream, if you like.

lime syrup Stir ingredients in small saucepan over low heat until sugar dissolves; bring to the boil. Boil, uncovered, 2 minutes or until syrup thickens slightly.

prep + cook time 1 hour 15 minutes serves 10

This cake has a lovely soft texture, thanks to the ricotta. The lime syrup adds a delicious tartness.

hazelnut mud cake with fudge frosting

360g dark chocolate, chopped coarsely

225g butter, chopped coarsely

¾ cup (165g) firmly packed brown sugar

¾ cup (180ml) water

¾ cup (110g) plain flour

¼ cup (35g) self-raising flour

½ cup (50g) hazelnut meal

2 eggs

⅓ cup (80ml) hazelnut-flavoured liqueur

FUDGE FROSTING

45g butter, chopped coarsely

1 tablespoon water

⅓ cup (75g) firmly packed brown sugar

2 tablespoons hazelnut-flavoured liqueur

1 cup (160g) icing sugar

2 tablespoons cocoa powder

tip We used Frangelico for this recipe, but you can use any hazelnut or chocolate-flavoured liqueur you like.

1 Preheat oven to 150°C/130°C fan-forced. Grease deep 20cm-round cake pan; line base and side with baking paper.

2 Combine chocolate, butter, sugar and the water in medium saucepan; stir over low heat until smooth. Cool 15 minutes.

3 Stir sifted flours, meal, eggs and liqueur into chocolate mixture. Pour mixture into pan; bake about 1 hour 35 minutes. Stand cake in pan 5 minutes before turning, top-side up, onto wire rack to cool.

4 Meanwhile, make fudge frosting. Spread cake with frosting.

fudge frosting Stir butter, the water and brown sugar in small saucepan over low heat until sugar dissolves. Remove from heat; stir in liqueur. Sift icing sugar and cocoa into small bowl; gradually stir in hot butter mixture until smooth. Cover, refrigerate about 15 minutes or until frosting thickens. Beat frosting with a wooden spoon until spreadable.

prep + cook time 2 hours (+ cooling) serves 12

125g butter, chopped coarsely

250g dark eating chocolate, chopped coarsely

⅔ cup (100g) self-raising flour

⅔ cup (150g) caster sugar

3 eggs

2 teaspoons finely grated orange rind

¼ cup (60ml) orange juice

2 tablespoons orange-flavoured liqueur

CHOC ORANGE GANACHE

200g dark eating chocolate, chopped

2 teaspoons finely grated orange rind

⅔ cup (160ml) cream

chocolate orange fudge cake

1 Preheat oven to 180°C/160°C fan-forced. Grease deep 20cm-round cake pan; line base and side with baking paper.

2 Combine butter and chocolate in medium saucepan; stir over low heat until smooth. Transfer to large bowl; cool 10 minutes.

3 Add sifted flour, sugar, eggs, rind, juice and liqueur to chocolate mixture; beat on low speed with electric mixer until ingredients are combined. Increase speed to medium; beat about 2 minutes or until mixture is smooth and paler in colour.

4 Pour mixture into pan; bake about 1 hour. Stand cake in pan 5 minutes before turning, top-side up, onto wire rack to cool.

5 Meanwhile, make choc orange ganache. Spread cake with ganache. Serve with whipped cream, if you like.

choc orange ganache Combine chocolate and rind in medium bowl. Bring cream to the boil in small saucepan. Add cream to chocolate mixture; stir until smooth. Stand 15 minutes or until ganache is spreadable.

prep + cook time 1 hour 15 minutes (+ standing) **serves** 10

tip We used Cointreau for this recipe but you can use any orange-flavoured liqueur you like.

baking tips

There's a lot to say about baking. We have referred to "cake" all the way through, but really we mean any baked goodies.

MEASURING

It's important to weigh and measure ingredients accurately to get consistently good results every time you bake — guesswork is not an option. We use standard metric cup and spoon measures; we give weights with most of our ingredients too, so you have the option to weigh or measure. If you're using cups and spoons, the ingredients are always leveled off with the flat blade of a table knife or metal spatula; the ingredients are shaken gently and loosely into the cups or spoons, not packed in, unless the recipe says so. We use a 250ml glass measuring jug for liquids; fill the jug to the required level, then check at eye level for accuracy. Australia is the only country in the world that uses a 20ml tablespoon. Make sure you check this before you buy the spoon set.

EQUIPMENT

BOWLS We prefer to use glass, china or stainless steel mixing bowls — you need a variety of sizes; small, medium and large. Wide-topped bowls are the easiest to use for hand-mixing.

WOODEN SPOONS Buy at least two medium-sized wooden spoons; keep them just for baking.

STRAINERS You need a sifter of some sort for sifting dry ingredients, a large fine plastic strainer will do the job. Small fine strainers are good for sifting small amounts of icing sugar or cocoa over cakes.

SPATULAS Plastic or rubber spatulas for scraping mixture from bowls etc., are a must, buy at least two.

SKEWERS Fine metal skewers are best for testing cakes.

WIRE RACKS Fine wire cake racks or coolers are used for cooling cakes. Buy two so you can turn cakes the right way up, gently sandwiching them between the two racks.

WHISKS A medium and a small balloon whisk are handy to have, but not essential, however, once you own a whisk or two, you'll be surprised at how much you'll use them.

ELECTRIC MIXERS

If you're serious about baking, buy a stand-alone mixer. A hand-held mixer will do the job well too, but it's boring holding the mixer. Blenders and food processors, both stand-alone and hand-held (also known as stab or wand mixers) are not suitable for normal cake-making.

OVENS

A good accurate oven is essential for consistent results. Always use the oven manufacturer's instructions as a guide to temperatures and oven positions. First, position the racks in the cold oven, make sure you have the racks the right way round and up — most racks have a raised end that goes at the back of the oven to stop pans sliding off, and most racks have a "stop" position that stops them sliding out of the oven or dipping down. Use the pans you're going to bake in to check they fit onto the shelves with space for heat to circulate and head-space for the cake to rise. As a general rule, the top of the baked cake should be in the centre of the oven. When the racks are correctly positioned, turn the oven to the correct temperature and mode.

Today, most domestic ovens are fan-forced; if you have a new oven of any type, be patient, make notes about cooking times and temperatures, so you can get used to how it works. Even the very best of ovens can be inaccurate, so have the thermostat calibrated by an expert, or buy an oven thermometer so you can check the temperature. It's vital that you get to know your oven well, some ovens have hot spots, so it might be necessary to change the positions of cakes around. Strictly speaking, fan-forced ovens should cook and brown cakes evenly everywhere and anywhere within the oven, but this is not always the case.

TESTING

The baking times we give in our recipes can only be used as a guide; there are too many factors beyond our control to give absolutely accurate baking times in any recipe. As you get towards the end of the baking time, open the oven door and have a look at the cake, if it's clearly nowhere near done, then close the oven door, re-set the timer to a new checking time. If you think the cake might be done, then touch the top of the cake with your fingers, gently but firmly enough to "feel" it. You should feel a crust and a firmness, and the cake should look like it might be wanting to pull away slightly from the side/s of the pan.

BUTTER CAKES Most butter cakes respond well to being tested with a fine metal skewer, do this while the cake is still in the oven, but with the rack slightly pulled out. Gently push the skewer through the thickest part of the cake, avoiding cracks, to the bottom of the pan. Gently withdraw the skewer, if you see cake mixture on the skewer, continue to bake the cake some more. If you don't see cake mixture, run your thumb and first finger down the skewer, and feel for any wet cake mixture, the skewer should come out of a cooked cake looking and feeling shiny and clean.

BROWNIES & MUD CAKES These are worth a special mention — even though one is a slice, and the other a kind of butter cake — because they can be tricky to get them to just the right texture. Both are usually made by a melt and mix method, and the recipes are always high in fat and sugar, so they often develop a sugary crust that can make testing difficult. Use a skewer for testing, as you would for a butter cake. Make a note of the time and temperature you use, so that you can turn them out with the texture you like best every time.

SPONGE CAKES Don't test a sponge cake with a skewer or it will deflate. Towards the end of the baking time, open the oven gently and have a look: it should be well-risen, browned, and not shrunken from the side of the pan. Gently feel the top of the sponge with your fingers, if it feels slightly firm, gently press your fingers onto the crust, your fingers should not leave any imprint. Have a wire rack ready, covered with baking paper.

Gently shake the pan to make sure the sponge is free from the base and side of the pan, then turn the sponge, top-side up, onto the wire rack.

FRUIT CAKES Those that contain a small to medium amount of fruit are really only butter cakes, so test them in the same way. Rich fruit cakes are best tested using the blade of a sharp pointed vegetable knife, the blade gives you a larger area to see and feel what's going on inside the cake. Be guided by the recipe's baking time, but always check about every half hour or so, they might need turning, or the top might be browning too much. If the correct-sized cake pan is used, and the lining done properly, the cake top should be protected from over-browning. Once you think the cake is cooked, feel the top with your fingers, there should be a feeling of a firm crust. Rich fruit cakes don't rise much — some recipes have no raising agent, others have only a little. Remove the cake from the oven, close the door, then gently push the blade of the knife into the centre of the cake, avoiding any cracks, down to the bottom of the pan. Gently pull the knife out of the cake, and look at the blade, if it has uncooked mixture on it, bake the cake some more. If the blade appears to be shiny and feels clean, just a little moist is fine, then the cake is done.

LOAVES & BREADS These are usually baked in narrow pans, such as bar, loaf or nut roll tins, they rise quickly and quite a lot. As a result, most loaf- and ring-shaped cakes crack along the centre. Test loaves and breads with a skewer, as you would a butter cake.

CUPCAKES, MUFFINS & FRIANDS All three cook quite quickly because of their size, so it's important not to overcook them. You can usually tell if they're cooked through, simply by looking at and touching them. If in doubt, use a skewer, as you would for a butter cake.

SLICES, BISCUITS & COOKIES The most important thing to remember is not to overcook them — they should develop a crust, but still feel slightly soft to the touch when you remove them from the oven. They will firm up as they cool to room temperature. The best test for biscuits and cookies is the "push" test. Using your thumb, gently push against an edge of a cookie or biscuit, if it's cooked, it will slide on the tray without breaking. Remove the tray from the oven, then follow the recipe for cooling.

SCONES Scones are easy to tell if they're done or not. They should be well-risen and even in colour. They don't take long to cook through, as they're small and are baked at a high temperature. The best test is to tap them with your finger, they have a quite distinctive "hollow" sound. Do this test on the scones in the centre of the batch, as the ones on the outside will have cooked first. Slide the scones onto a wire rack and cover them loosely to cool.

THE LAST WORD

The first time you use a recipe, read it all the way through then, when you make the recipe, make notes next to it — these notes are a good reference to have the next time you make the recipe.

cake pans

Cakes pans are made from many different materials, and come in a variety of shapes and sizes. Your baking results will be affected by the cake pans you use, read below for the finer points.

Once upon a time, cake pans were made from tin of varying qualities, and aluminium without any coating, but now they're made from a huge range of materials of many different qualities. Price is usually your best guide to quality and, with proper care, your cake pans should last you a long time. However, if you have any uncoated aluminium cake pans, hang on to them, as aluminium is a wonderful conductor of heat. Silicone "pans" are also becoming increasingly popular as they are durable and user-friendly. The material distributes heat evenly and cools down quickly once out of the oven; again, as with other types of pans, price is a good guide to quality.

PAN SIZES

There are many different brands, shapes, depths and sizes of cake pans on the market. All the pans we used throughout this book are readily available in supermarkets, department stores, chain stores, homeware shops and specialty food and kitchen stores. We've listed and pictured (*see opposite page*) most of the pans we've used in this book. A lot of the new, coated pans have wide overhanging rims for easy handling; these are helpful for removing hot pans from the oven. We've found the way cake pan manufacturer's measure their pans doesn't always agree with ours, so if buying specific-sized cake pans, take your tape measure so you can measure the pans before buying them.

GREASING PANS

These days, most pans are coated with a non-stick finish, however, despite this, we suggest that you grease the pans with a light, even coating of cooking-oil spray to be sure the cakes will turn out easily. We found the same greasing rules applied to silicone pans too. If the surface of the pans is scratched, then it's vital to grease the pans thoroughly. Sometimes we line the base of the cake pans too, and sometimes the side/s as well. We suggest using melted butter for greasing heavily patterned pans, such as baba pans. Nut roll tins deserve a special mention; we found melted butter to be the best for these tins.

FILLING THE PANS

A lot of the new pans have sloping sides, which means that the capacity will be slightly less than straight-sided pans; allow for this when you're filling the cake pans, and be aware that baking times might be slightly reduced because there will be less mixture. Most butter cakes will double in size during baking; rich fruit cakes will hardly rise at all; and sponges should triple in size, so allow for this when you're filling a pan with cake mixture. Because there is a lot of variation in the depths of pans, as a guide, fill pans two-thirds to three-quarters with butter cake mixtures; half-fill pans with sponge mixtures; rich fruit cake mixtures hardly rise, so the pans can

be filled almost to the brim. You also need to consider the shape of the pan as well. Cake mixtures baked in slab, slice, lamington or baking dishes will rise less than those baked in loaf, bar or ring-shaped pans. Using an incorrect sized or shaped cake pan will cause you grief. The best advice of all is to stick to the recipe and use the size and shape of pan we suggest.

COOKING PROPERTIES

In this book we have reduced baking temperatures by 10°C to compensate for the use of non-stick coated cake pans; cakes baked in these pans need to be baked at a lower temperature than those baked in uncoated aluminium pans. Also, the colour and thickness of the cake's crust will vary according to what type of cake pan is used for baking. Silicone pans develop the softest and lightest-coloured crust of all. Uncoated aluminium develops an even, golden crust, and the rest of the pans — including non-stick coated pans, tin and stainless steel pans — all develop heavier, darker crusts. Some of the new cake pans have removable bases; these are good, providing the base fits tightly. If you're in doubt about the fit, cover the base section with foil, overlapping the side slightly, then position the base in the pan. When using new cake pans for the first time, it's best to make a note of the oven temperature and baking time on the recipe for future reference.

1 deep 20cm-square loose-based cake pan 2 deep 20cm-square cake pan 3 shallow 22cm-round cake pan 4 shallow 20cm-round cake pan 5 12-hole (½-cup/125ml) oval friand pan 6 12-hole (2-tablespoons/40ml) flat-based patty pan 7 12-hole (1-tablespoon/20ml) mini muffin pan 8 24-hole (1-tablespoon/20ml) silicone mini muffin pan 9 8cm x 20cm nut roll tin (20cm with lids on) 10 deep 20cm-round cake pan 11 6-hole (¾-cup/180ml) texas muffin pan 12 12-hole ($^{1}/_{3}$-cup/80ml) muffin pan 13 12cm x 22cm loaf pan 14 6-hole (¾ cup/180ml) fluted tube pan 15 shallow 22cm-square cake pan 16 22cm x 32cm rectangular cake pan 17 12-hole (1½-tablespoons/30ml) round-based patty pans 18 8-hole (¾-cup/180ml) petite loaf pan 19 deep 20cm ring pan 20 deep 23cm-round cake pan 21 20cm silicone baba pan 22 19cm x 30cm lamington pan 23 24cm x 32cm swiss roll pan 24 26.5cm x 36.5cm (16-cup/4-litre) baking dish.

Glossary

ALMOND a flat, pointy-ended nut with a creamy white kernel that is covered by a brown skin.
meal also known as finely ground almonds; powdered to a flour-like texture and used in baking or as a thickening agent.

BACON RASHERS also known as slices.

BAKING POWDER a raising agent consisting of two parts cream of tartar to one part bicarbonate of soda. The acid and alkaline combination, when moistened and heated, gives off carbon dioxide, which aerates and lightens the mixture during baking.

BEETROOT also known as red beets or beets; firm, round root vegetable.

BICARBONATE OF SODA also known as baking or carb soda; a mild alkali used as a leavening agent in baking.

BISCUITS also known as cookies.
butternut snap a crunchy biscuit made with golden syrup, oats and coconut.
chocolate-chip cookies plain biscuits with pieces (or chips) of chocolate.
plain chocolate a crisp sweet biscuit with added cocoa powder but with no icing or filling.

BREAD, MOUNTAIN a thin flat, dry, soft-textured bread; can be rolled up and filled with your favourite filling.

BUTTER use salted or unsalted (sweet) butter; 125g is equal to one stick (4 ounces) of butter.
unsalted butter has no added salt, and is often called 'sweet' butter. The salt content of regular salted butter is sometimes discernable in a sweet recipe, especially with chocolate. You can use regular butter in most cakes and baking, but it's advisable to stick to unsalted butter when it's specified in delicate toppings, icings and so on.

BUTTERMILK originally the term given to the slightly sour liquid left after butter was churned from cream, today it is commercially made similarly to yogurt. Sold alongside all fresh milk products in supermarkets; despite the implication of its name, it's low in fat.

CAPSICUM also known as bell pepper or, simply, pepper. Be sure to discard seeds and membranes before use. Roasted capsicum is also available, bottled in oil or brine, from most supermarkets and delicatessens.

CARAMEL TOP 'N' FILL a delicious caramel filling made from milk and cane sugar. It can be used straight from the can for slices, tarts and cheesecakes. Has similar qualities to sweetened condensed milk.

CAYENNE PEPPER a thin-fleshed, long, extremely hot red chilli; usually purchased dried and ground.

CHEESE
bocconcini walnut-sized, delicate, semi-soft fresh baby mozzarella. The name derives from the diminutive of 'boccone' meaning mouthful. Spoils rapidly so keep under refrigeration, in brine, for two days at most.
brie often referred to as the 'queen of cheeses'. Has a bloomy white rind and a creamy centre that becomes runnier as it ripens.
cream commonly known as Philly or Philadelphia, a soft, cows-milk cheese. Also available as a spreadable light cream cheese, which is a blend of cottage and cream cheeses.
fetta a crumbly goat- or sheep-milk cheese with a sharp salty taste.
parmesan also known as parmigiano, a hard, grainy, cows-milk cheese.
pizza a blend of grated mozzarella, cheddar and parmesan cheeses.

ricotta a sweet, moist, white, cows-milk cheese with a slightly grainy texture. Its name roughly translates as 'cooked again'. Made from whey, a by-product of other cheese-making, to which fresh milk and acid are added.

CHIVES related to the onion and leek; has a subtle onion flavour.

CHOCOLATE
Choc Bits also known as chocolate chips and chocolate morsels; available in milk, white and dark chocolate. These hold their shape in baking and are ideal for decorating.
chocolate Melts discs of compounded dark, milk or white chocolate ideal for melting and moulding.
dark eating also known as semi-sweet or luxury chocolate; made from a high percentage of cocoa liquor and cocoa butter, and a little added sugar.
milk eating most popular eating chocolate; mild and very sweet.
white eating contains no cocoa solids but derives its sweet flavour from cocoa butter. Very sensitive to heat so watch carefully if melting.

COCOA POWDER also known as cocoa; dried, unsweetened, roasted then ground cocoa beans.

CONFECTIONERY
boiled lollies a thick paste of boiled sugar and water to which colour and flavourings are added before the mixture is rolled and cut into pieces and hardened. Also known as rock candy, humbugs and bulleyes.
chocolate lady beetle or bee these novelty chocolates are moulded into various shapes then wrapped in a colourful identifying foil.
fruit allsort a type of licorice allsort.
jelly baby very small jelly-type lollies in the shape of a baby.

Mars Bar a chocolate nougat bar topped with a layer of caramel and covered with milk chocolate.

mint leaves soft jelly lolly with a minty colour and flavour, shaped into a small leaf.

Smartie popular small, round, sugar-coated chocolate confectionery.

CORELLA PEARS miniature dessert pears up to 10cm long.

CORNFLOUR known as cornstarch; used as a thickening agent in all types of cooking.

wheaten cornflour made from wheat rather than corn – gives sponge cakes a lighter texture (due to the fact wheaten cornflour has some gluten).

CRANBERRIES, DRIED have the same slightly sour, succulent flavour as fresh cranberries. Available in most supermarkets and health-food stores.

CREAM we use fresh cream, also known as pure cream and pouring cream, unless otherwise stated. Minimum fat content 35%.

sour a thick, cultured soured cream. Minimum fat content 35%.

thickened whipping cream containing a thickener. Minimum fat content 35%.

CREAM OF TARTAR acid ingredient in baking powder; added to confectionery mixtures to help prevent sugar from crystallising. Keeps frostings creamy and improves volume when beating egg whites.

CUMIN also known as zeera or comino; resembling caraway in size, cumin is the dried seed of a plant related to the parsley family having a spicy, nutty flavour. Available in seed form or dried and ground.

CURRANTS, DRIED tiny, almost black raisins so-named after a grape variety that originated in Corinth, Greece.

CUSTARD POWDER instant mixture used to make pouring custard; similar to North American instant pudding mixes.

DAIRY-FREE SPREAD also known as dairy-free margarine. We used Diet Becel, a commercial product having a fat content of 2.4g per 5g of spread.

FLOUR

plain an all-purpose flour made from wheat.

rice a very fine flour made from ground white rice.

self-raising plain flour sifted with baking powder in the proportion of 1 cup flour to 2 teaspoons baking powder. Also available gluten-free from most supermarkets.

wholemeal also known as whole wheat flour. Flour milled from the whole wheat grain (bran and germ).

FOOD COLOURING a digestible substance used to give colour to food, can be made from vegetable dyes and is available in liquid or powdered form.

FRUIT MINCE also known as mincemeat. A mixture of dried fruits such as raisins, sultanas and candied peel, nuts, spices, apple, brandy or rum. Is used as a filling for cakes, puddings and fruit mince pies.

FRUIT, MIXED DRIED a combination of sultanas, raisins, currants, mixed peel and cherries.

GINGER also green or root ginger; the thick root of a tropical plant.

glacé fresh ginger root preserved in sugar syrup. Crystallised ginger can be substituted if rinsed with warm water and dried before using.

ground also known as powdered ginger; used as a flavouring in cakes, pies and puddings but cannot be substituted for fresh ginger.

GLACÉ FRUIT fruit that has been preserved in a sugar syrup.

GOLDEN SYRUP a by-product of refined sugar cane; pure maple syrup or honey can be substituted.

HAZELNUTS also known as filberts; plump, grape-size, rich, sweet nut having a brown inedible skin that is removed by rubbing heated nuts together vigorously in a tea towel.

meal also known as ground hazelnuts.

JAM also as preserve or conserve.

JELLY CRYSTALS a powdered mixture of gelatine, sweetener and artificial fruit flavouring that's used to make a moulded, translucent, quivering dessert. Also known as jello.

LEMON CURD a smooth spread, usually made from lemons, butter and eggs.

LEMON THYME a herb with a lemony scent, which is due to the high level of citral — an oil also found in lemon, orange, verbena and lemon grass — in its leaves. The citrus scent is enhanced by crushing the leaves in your hands before using the herb.

LIQUEURS use your favourite brand of liqueur, if preferred.

coffee-flavoured we use Kahlúa or Tia Maria.

hazelnut-flavoured we use Frangelico.

orange-flavoured we use Cointreau, Curaçao or Grand Marnier.

LOLLIES confectionery; also known as sweets or candy.

MAPLE SYRUP a thin syrup distilled from the sap of the maple tree. Maple-flavoured syrup or pancake syrup is not an adequate substitute for the real thing.

MARMALADE a preserve, usually based on citrus fruit.

MINCE also known as ground meat.

MIXED SPICE a blend of spices that is generally used in sweet dishes such as fruit cakes, shortbread biscuits and fruit pies.

MUESLI also known as granola; a combination of grains (mainly oats), nuts and dried fruits.

MUSTARD, DIJON also known as french mustard. Pale brown, creamy, distinctively flavoured, fairly mild french mustard.

NUTS, TOASTING/ROASTING To toast nuts, place shelled, peeled nuts, in a single layer, in small dry frying pan; cook, over low heat, until fragrant and just changed in colour. To roast, spread in a single layer on oven tray; roast in a moderate oven for about 10 minutes or until golden. Be careful to avoid burning nuts.

OATS, ROLLED oat groats (oats that have been husked) steamed-softened, flattened with rollers, dried and packaged as a cereal product.

ONIONS, GREEN also known as scallion or, incorrectly, shallot; an immature onion picked before the bulb has formed, having a long, bright-green edible stalk.

PARSLEY, FLAT-LEAF also known as continental or italian parsley.

PEPITAS dried pumpkin seeds.

PINE NUTS also known as pignoli.

PISTACHIOS pale green, delicately flavoured nut inside hard off-white shells. To peel, soak shelled nuts in boiling water for about 5 minutes; drain, then pat dry with absorbent paper. Rub skins with a cloth to peel.

PROSCIUTTO a kind of unsmoked Italian ham; salted, air-cured and aged, it is usually eaten uncooked.

QUINCE yellow-skinned fruit with a hard texture and astringent, tart taste; eaten cooked or as a preserve. Quince paste is available from specialist food stores and some delicatessens.

RAISINS dried sweet grapes.

REDCURRANT JELLY a preserve made from redcurrants; used as a glaze for desserts and meats, or in sauces.

RHUBARB has thick, celery-like stalks that can reach up to 60cm long; the stalks are the only edible portion of the plant — the leaves contain a toxic substance. Though generally eaten as a fruit, rhubarb is a vegetable.

RUM, DARK we prefer to use an underproof rum (not overproof) for a more subtle flavour.

SAUCE, BARBECUE a spicy, tomato-based sauce used to marinate or baste, or as a condiment.

SEMOLINA made from durum wheat milled into various textured granules, all of these finer than flour; it is available from health-food stores and some major supermarkets. Semolina can be replaced (weight for weight) with plain flour.

SPINACH also known as english spinach and, incorrectly, silver beet.

SUGAR

brown a soft, finely granulated sugar retaining molasses (a thick dark syrup produced from sugar cane) for its characteristic colour and flavour.

caster also known as superfine or finely granulated table sugar.

dark brown a moist sugar with a rich distinctive full flavour coming from natural molasses syrup. It is ideal for sweetening fruits, puddings and fruit cakes, gingerbread or chocolate cakes, adding both colour and flavour.

icing also known as confectioners' sugar or powdered sugar; granulated sugar crushed together with a small amount of cornflour added.

icing pure also known as confectioners' sugar or powdered sugar. Has no added cornflour.

SULTANAS dried grapes, also known as golden raisins.

SWEETENED CONDENSED MILK a canned milk product consisting of milk with more than half the water content removed and sugar added to the remaining milk.

TOMATO

cherry also known as tiny tim or tom thumb; a small, round tomato.

paste triple-concentrated tomato purée used to flavour soups, stews, sauces and casseroles.

pasta sauce a prepared sauce made from tomatoes, herbs and spices.

sun-dried tomato pesto a thick paste made from sun-dried tomatoes, oil, vinegar and herbs.

TREACLE a concentrated syrup with a distinctive flavour and dark black colour; a by-product of sugar refining.

VANILLA

bean dried long, thin pod from a tropical golden orchid; the tiny black seeds impart a luscious vanilla flavour in baking and desserts.

extract vanilla beans that have been submerged in alcohol. Vanilla essence is not a suitable substitute.

VEGEMITE Australia's favourite sandwich spread — made from leftover brewers' yeast extract, the taste may be described as salty, slightly bitter and malty. If you can't find it, substitute with Marmite.

ZUCCHINI also known as courgette.

Conversion chart

MEASURES

One Australian metric measuring cup holds approximately 250ml; one Australian metric tablespoon holds 20ml; one Australian metric teaspoon holds 5ml.

The difference between one country's measuring cups and another's is within a two- or three-teaspoon variance, and will not affect your cooking results. North America, New Zealand and the United Kingdom use a 15ml tablespoon.

All cup and spoon measurements are level. The most accurate way of measuring dry ingredients is to weigh them. When measuring liquids, use a clear glass or plastic jug with the metric markings.

We use large eggs with an average weight of 60g.

DRY MEASURES

METRIC	IMPERIAL
15g	½oz
30g	1oz
60g	2oz
90g	3oz
125g	4oz (¼lb)
155g	5oz
185g	6oz
220g	7oz
250g	8oz (½lb)
280g	9oz
315g	10oz
345g	11oz
375g	12oz (¾lb)
410g	13oz
440g	14oz
470g	15oz
500g	16oz (1lb)
750g	24oz (1½lb)
1kg	32oz (2lb)

LIQUID MEASURES

METRIC	IMPERIAL
30ml	1 fluid oz
60ml	2 fluid oz
100ml	3 fluid oz
125ml	4 fluid oz
150ml	5 fluid oz (¼ pint/1 gill)
190ml	6 fluid oz
250ml	8 fluid oz
300ml	10 fluid oz (½ pint)
500ml	16 fluid oz
600ml	20 fluid oz (1 pint)
1000ml (1 litre)	1¾ pints

LENGTH MEASURES

METRIC	IMPERIAL
3mm	⅛in
6mm	¼in
1cm	½in
2cm	¾in
2.5cm	1in
5cm	2in
6cm	2½in
8cm	3in
10cm	4in
13cm	5in
15cm	6in
18cm	7in
20cm	8in
23cm	9in
25cm	10in
28cm	11in
30cm	12in (1ft)

OVEN TEMPERATURES

These oven temperatures are only a guide for conventional ovens. For fan-forced ovens, check the manufacturer's manual.

	°C (CELSIUS)	°F (FAHRENHEIT)	GAS MARK
Very slow	120	250	½
Slow	150	275-300	1-2
Moderately slow	160	325	3
Moderate	180	350-375	4-5
Moderately hot	200	400	6
Hot	220	425-450	7-8
Very hot	240	475	9

Index

ACP BOOKS

General manager Christine Whiston
Editor-in-chief Susan Tomnay
Creative director Hieu Chi Nguyen
Art director & designer Hannah Blackmore
Senior editor Wendy Bryant
Food writer Xanthe Roberts
Food director Pamela Clark
Test Kitchen manager Belinda Farlow
Recipe development Belinda Farlow; Cathie Lonnie
Sales & rights director Brian Cearnes
Marketing manager Bridget Cody
Senior business analyst Rebecca Varela
Circulation manager Jarna Mclean
Operations manager David Scotto
Production manager Victoria Jefferys

ACP Books are published by ACP Magazines a division of PBL Media Pty Limited
PBL Media, Chief Executive Officer Ian Law
Publishing & sales director, Women's lifestyle Lynette Phillips
Group editorial director, Women's lifestyle Pat Ingram
Marketing director, Women's lifestyle Matthew Dominello
Commercial manager, Women's lifestyle Seymour Cohen
Research director, Women's lifestyle Justin Stone

Produced by ACP Books, Sydney.

Published by ACP Books, a division of ACP Magazines Ltd, 54 Park St, Sydney; GPO Box 4088, Sydney, NSW 2001.
phone (02) 9282 8618; fax (02) 9267 9438; acpbooks@acpmagazines.com.au; www.acpbooks.com.au

Printed by Dai Nippon in Korea.

Australia Distributed by Network Services,
phone +61 2 9282 8777; fax +61 2 9264 3278; networkweb@networkservicescompany.com.au
United Kingdom Distributed by Australian Consolidated Press (UK),
phone (01604) 642 200; fax (01604) 642 300; books@acpuk.com
New Zealand Distributed by Netlink Distribution Company,
phone (9) 366 9966; ask@ndc.co.nz
South Africa Distributed by PSD Promotions,
phone (27 11) 392 6065/6/7; fax (27 11) 392 6079/80; orders@psdprom.co.za
Canada Distributed by Publishers Group Canada
phone (800) 663 5714; fax (800) 565 3770; service@raincoast.com

Title: Easy baking / food director Pamela Clark.
ISBN: 978 186396 863 8 (pbk.)
Notes: Includes index.
Subjects: Baking.
Other Authors/Contributors Clark, Pamela.
Dewey Number: 641.815
© ACP Magazines Ltd 2009 ABN 18 053 273 546
Scanpan cookware is used in the AWW Test Kitchen.

The publishers would like to thank the following for props used in photography: Dinosaur Designs, Essential Ingredient,
Maxwell & Williams, Miljö, Mud Australia, Top3 By Design, Waterford Wedgwood.

Send recipe enquiries to: recipeenquiries@acpmagazines.com.au